a way of knowing

joy mead is a member of the Iona Community and the author of *The One Loaf*, *A Telling Place*, *Making Peace in Practice and Poetry*, *Where Are the Altars?* and *Words and Wonderings*. She leads creative writing groups, and has been involved in development education and justice and peace work.

a way of knowing

Joy Mead

wild goose
publications

www.ionabooks.com

Published 2012 by
Wild Goose Publications
Fourth Floor, Savoy House, 140 Sauchiehall Street, Glasgow G2 3DH, UK,
the publishing division of the Iona Community.
Scottish Charity No. SC003794.
Limited Company Reg. No. SC096243.

ISBN 978-1-84952-223-6

Cover artwork: StephenRaw.com © 2012

The publishers gratefully acknowledge the support of The Drummond Trust, 3 Pitt Terrace, Stirling FK8 2EY in producing this book.

A catalogue record for this book is available from the British Library.

Overseas distribution:
N. America: Novalis/Bayard, 10 Lower Spadina Ave., Suite 400, Toronto, Ontario M5V 2Z
Australia: Willow Connection Pty Ltd, Unit 4A, 3-9 Kenneth Road, Manly Vale, NSW 2093
New Zealand: Pleroma Christian Supplies, Higginson St., Otane 4170, Central Hawkes Bay

Printed by Bell & Bain,
Thornliebank, Glasgow, UK

contents

Part two Seeing

Part three Sharing

a way of knowing

The heightened colours
in an ordinary room
where a child sleeps,
empty bowls on the table,
a turning dial
on a washing machine,
the old man who waits
for tomorrow's sun,
the star that fell from an envelope
my grandsons gave me at Christmas,
cabbages in an organic garden,
lights in my neighbour's window,
gannets over the sea,
dolphins in the sound
on a day of delight,
a boat under a tarpaulin,
the words of a prayer
taken out of the ordinary
run of language,
a pile of stones, waiting
like the words of a poem
for the hands
that will guide them,
the lasting colour
of birch leaves
at the end of autumn,

the handful of seeds
and the mouthful of bread
that make despair impossible.

A way of being and placing,
seeing and naming,

that holds the intensity
of the moment,
cherishing it,

playing the music of dailyness
through all remembering:
a way to the intelligence
of the heart.

beginnings

We're not short of information and there's no doubt that readily available facts and figures, data and statistics are useful to us. We need them, but not to excess – a few will often do! At the same time, we have to recognise that so much of what is essential for wholeness of life can never be measured or known in any quantifiable or scientific sense. Love and compassion lie in the realm of the unquantifiable, and so does our response to beauty, and to the natural world around us when we are not busy measuring its usefulness.

Alongside our intellectual knowledge exists that quiet wisdom, in its own place, which is indigenous knowledge. We need such imagination, discernment, understanding, perception. So much of this kind of knowing comes initially through our senses (our awareness, our attentiveness to things, how we look and see, listen and hear, touch and respond); it comes through our experiences, through our relationships with others, with our earth, or maybe through story, poetry, music, song and sounds. We don't absorb significant experiences as abstractions – we take them personally. They are written on our bodies. They are particular to us but often become universal in the sharing, the telling. For all experience is valid. Each story has significance: it will almost inevitably be about what we value – how we celebrate the values we live by, how we experience the challenges to those values. Through our stories (however expressed) we learn about our struggles, we tell of our experience and we begin to understand ourselves. Sharing the story of who we are and what we have seen, and listening to the stories of others: these are amongst the greatest things we do in our time on earth.

I wonder what this might mean for us in the twenty-first century in terms of what we still call 'worship', although I often wonder, too, what we think we mean by that word and by the way we use worship space. Isn't worship, after all, gathering to rejoice and to grieve, to celebrate and to lament? It's struggling to find a way to express what it means to be alive and to be human. It's bringing people to one another, into knowing and into unknowing.

So, for me, worship has to be about poetry … and theology maybe, but in the end they are much the same. Poetry is more than a particular arrangement of words on a page. It's a way of being, a way of seeing and a way of knowing. It's about awareness and consciousness, being fully alive in all our experiences. Poetry is not a vehicle for ideas. It shows what we have touched and seen and heard. Through poetry we find our own story to live by.

I hope that *A Way of Knowing* might be a book to use not just *in* worship but to encourage different approaches to and understandings of worship: an exploration not only of what we do but of how we think, the words we use and how they might be received by others. This would mean seeking to make the worship space bigger, much bigger, so that we look at *how* we experience all life and bring our seeing to such a space.

By this, I don't mean thinking about projects but rather creating a blessed or sacred empty space into which all life might flow. I'm looking for something viable to replace what is no longer working for so many people. In the actual physical space paper might be unfurled for painting. A film might be projected onto a wall. Music might be played. Some might write or cook or sew or plant. There could be drama created out of whatever is at hand – objects and emotions … all our concerns, what we value, our anger and our compassion – and, through this creativity, reality might be transformed.

Any communication between human bodies means that the nature of the moment continually changes: from sadness to joy, from lament to celebration, from seriousness to humour. When everything becomes too intense, people might move back to the edges and allow their own sorrow or joy to be poured into the space they have created, the place of thoughts, hopes and memories. The way we seek to express our sense of loss and what we value will move us towards the overflowing silence, towards what can never be known, towards the peace that comes with not needing to know. Silence, emptiness, uncertainty will be celebrated rather than feared … and food will be quietly shared.

Now, I realise that the possibility of all this *actually, physically happening* is fairly remote, but if it takes place in our minds, in our dreams, then that's something! The sharing space is a dreamtime. It's how we feel, as well as what we do. It might be seen as waiting upon life.

This isn't about worship seen as meeting God or finding God or even praising God (for the concept of a God who continually needs to be praised raises its own questions) but about coming to an understanding of living which arises from experience, perception, looking, seeing, understanding, thinking and memory … walking *humbly with* our God, no more, no less …

In this way, we would really be paying attention (that greatest form of generosity), both individually and as a group, to what is happening in our church, our community, our country, our world. We would ask difficult questions and go on asking them. An eyes-open approach might begin with the need to lament … and move from there to hope … and then to speaking out. We know that there are too many good people keeping quiet just now.

We need to be prepared to ask questions that are not academic or scientific or logical but personal. We need to be prepared to make fools of ourselves! There may be no answers, but often change depends on the questions we ask.

This book has three sections containing various writings

around the knowledge/wisdom theme: how we come to know, how we understand, how we live with our unknowing and our uncertainty. I had already written several *What I know about …* poems and for a long time I've thought about seeds and seed-saving. Now I'm beginning to make the connections: the poet as seed-sower/seed-saver; the way we come upon knowledge, which is not about accumulation of information but something much more organic – nebulous, mysterious even, saved, shared and passed on, and at one with the intricate dance of earth, air, fire, water.

There are three sections with one theme but slight variations. You will see that they overlap. That's inevitable. The poems and pieces could be interchangeable – the sections interact. It's how you read that will matter. Each section contains what might look like (but isn't!) a random selection of poetry, reflection, liturgy, stories and articles. The introductions to sections won't necessarily refer in any detail to the pieces and poems but will give an idea of what they are trying to do.

I hope you will be led to think about what words, actions, gifts, concerns and other attributes you might bring to the sacred space, and what the space means, not as a gathering set aside from day-to-day activity but as people together understanding the wonder of ordinary life and how to share it. The authority – if that is the right word – is yours and mine.

part one

looking

poetry

like the flight of a bird
caught in the sunlight
then disappearing into the trees:
something seen and re-created
made known
for always.

looking

What we most remember of life is its poetry and we, rather than canon-makers or theologians, determine the relationship between our ordinary day-to-day living and what we attempt to express in poetry (or theology). What, after all, is the point of art or tradition if it silences new experiences … if it silences *my* experience …?

Poetry has the power to dignify the everyday things and the ordinary people of our lives. The authority of the poet is to show significance, value, beauty; to show how a thing makes its own importance. We are surrounded by objects and imagery. What we put on the walls of our homes, our churches, the images we use in our public places, our sacred spaces, matter. We live by imagery and imagination. Images are not ornaments. Like language itself they make our lives. The objects in a room can be instructive if *we* give them meaning, if we absorb into a new understanding the wisdom of tradition and older learning. Nothing is fixed and unchangeable. We must go to the past with the same ability to see and listen as we approach the present.

So let's begin with particulars, even what might be seen as sentimental or mundane. Mother's necklace, the pen on my desk, grandfather's cap, a child's first shoes, a book left on a bench, the sounds of the washing machine, morning sun on the bricks of home, the feel of the new beech leaves, the touch of a peach on your tongue, the warm glow of wood, picnics and pies, cow parsley, the scent of warm grass, the red of strawberries, the sound of a ringing rock, windblown summer chairs, washing lines – and connections between things: a stone and an abbey, a web and a friendship, peace and a prehistoric settlement, a boat and death, scissors and the trade union movement. Things together make our lives. They tell who we are.

Poetry isn't ideas; it's experiences. On the whole, abstractions don't make for vivid poetic writing. Try to write about the meaning of life and you're likely to come up against a stone wall. Write about a stone wall and you might just touch upon the meaning of life. To write, tell, express in whatever medium you choose can't be abstract. It must be grounded. If you think you *know* before you *look* then you won't *see*.

Isn't it one of the great cruelties of Alzheimer's that it's things that are lost? The nouns die first. Things, as in a memory box, are the way into our stories: all the colours of all the seasons of our lives will be in our minds, understood through memories.

To be human is to know through our senses, through the body and its immediate horizon, when the small world and the epic world become inseparable in a remaking of poetry and theology: a home place of body and mind. 'Home' is when you 'know' a place with all your being through its constituent parts: fields of grass, trees and tracks, distinctive buildings, particular places and plants, the smell left in a coat. Home is the moment you live in fully. Telling your story – the particulars of place and time, the insight and intimacy of everyday objects and actions – this is homecoming.

Jesus, you might remember, liked things – coins and clay, bread and boats, fish and fruits – and the people around them: carpenters and children, fishermen, farmers and food-servers.

So much is about small things and little occasions, about smells, colours, sounds, touch and the looking and the love that make them significant.

what i know about place

is that when Iona Abbey was a ruin
sea spleenwort took root on the south wall
above the choir where it can't be missed.

The wall is no longer exposed
to sun, sky, rain or sea salt wind,
but the sea spleenwort continues
to grow, to thrive

to know its place and time
remarkably well.

feet on the ground

When my first grandchild, William, was born, the midwife said that he had the biggest feet she had ever seen on a newborn baby. I recognised the size and shape of those feet – I could see that he belonged! He will, I hope, have those distinctive feet set firmly, but lightly, on the earth – sure-footed in the ground of his own understanding.

Elizabeth, my daughter, and I took William to visit his great-grandmother who was in her nineties. It was a moving experience – the look of pure wonder and delight in her eyes matched that in William's. There was a sense of resurrection. Faced with a new beginning, new growing life, she seemed young again. Hope – the tomorrow she wouldn't see – was there in her arms and she was part of it.

Rootedness, belonging, hope – all there in the Christmas story, as down to earth as you can get. Angels, kings, shepherds and animals all play their part in reminding us of the wonder, mystery and earthiness of new life.

I remember a minister friend, annoyed, telling me that a crying baby had interrupted his carol service. That wasn't an interruption, I thought, that was the flesh and blood heart of the service. So I have never been able to get my mind around that line in *Away in a Manger*: 'Little Lord Jesus, no crying he makes'.

The Christmas story roots us firmly in this world: the baby in the manger comes into the world of the here and now, the daily fight against dirt, the daily struggle for food, water and shelter, the daily confrontation with sickness and death ... a world of power struggles and tyranny ... but also a world of beauty and wonder where life is given, sustained and handed on.

Incarnation is a good word. It's about the glory and holiness of flesh and blood, about how we value life. The same question asked in the Christmas story is asked for every baby born: 'What will this child be?'

We understand most things on our bodies first: remember the wordless communication between my grandson and his great-grandmother; remember that lovely line from Christina Rossetti's carol *In the Bleak Midwinter*: 'But only his mother/In her maiden bliss/Worshipped the beloved/With a kiss.' Then we begin to make sense of what we feel, or perhaps we just rest with the mystery. When Mary's baby was born, she pondered things in her heart – she didn't write a book of theology.

'Listen, I will unfold a mystery' – Paul's words in 1 Corinthians 15:51 – is still a powerful message: that we can love – and go on loving against the greatest odds, beyond all reason. That is the light that shines in the dark days of December.

Do you remember that scene in *Only Fools and Horses* when Del Boy's baby is born. He holds the child up to show Rodney. 'What is it?' Rodney asks. Del Boy, with a look of wonder, mystery and pure joy, says, 'It's a li'l baby.' If you understand that then you're beginning to understand what Christmas is about. Don't let anyone tell you different.

christmas child

December dark, and what awaits
our attempts at imagery
is not to be found
in the unmaking
of any ice-cold metaphor
but is an ecstasy, a beginning
of thought, released
by a light we cherish
in the eyes of every child
newborn.

recognising the gift

A misplaced cornerstone
catches the early sun,
unmossed in its place,
an overspent adjective
in an average sentence,
gathering a different story,
something in brackets,
a surprising insert
into an ordinary day.

It stops us in our tracks,
leaves us puzzled but recognising
that what might have been an Abbey stone
has, like belief and trust,
appropriately settled
somewhere else.

straight lines are overrated (or the particularity of stones)

1.

The unworking parts
of a dismantled clock
may be a mocking reminder
of our foolish attempts
to measure time,
to make it serve
in lines from then to now,
straight and true.
The clock has stopped,
its parts unworking,
its question hanging in the air.
Its question hangs in the air.

2.

A place of circles
stands the test of time.
Wind touches the particularity
of stones and sings the years
of their being here.

With grass and stars,
rainbows and butterflies,
they hold their peace
along with doubts and dreams,
in a question perfectly suspended:
calendar, clock or altar?

We may never know
and yet between us
and the stones
warm in the sun
is an inexpressible relationship.

Here the time is ours.

Poetry is about time – carpe diem being one of its oldest themes – and it's about time running out, ending in death. That is the journey. What could be closer to our common human experience? The journey is universal in concept and particular in our understanding. That's where the poetry, the storytelling, comes in.

in a cottage garden
(for Catherine, with love)

Old-fashioned flowers blossom
like love and memory,
intertwining with part of a story
just beginning.

In the last light of the day,
I'm remembering a girl
learning to be adult, carrying
in one enormous rucksack
more than I could lift
in a lifetime
and I see her shadow
walking on
past the lighted windows
of the cottage
where you are now
a young woman
at home.

going home

She was never dying,
my mother, on her feet
one moment, the next
gone. Where? How far?
What was in her mind
that last hour, last minute,
standing late at night
in a hospital ward
almost alone.

And I, unable to sleep
twenty miles away, anticipating
the next day's journey
the longest of both our lives
ending we thought
in a place of care.

She, entirely in character,
with urgency
and immaculate timing
chose a different way
home.

a parable of things and earthiness

In the winter of 1850, a wild storm stripped the grass from high dunes on the Bay of Skaill, Mainland Orkney, and revealed the ruins of a village around five thousand years old, inhabited before the Egyptian pyramids were built. It was Skara Brae, a community that flourished before construction began at Stonehenge.

Skara Brae is an entrancing place, remarkable for more than its age. Sun, sea, wind and rain touch innocent patterns of survival and sharing – a prehistoric housing scheme with a pattern of daily activities. It's a celebration of domestic life. The houses are open to the sky now and as you stand at roof level you look down upon passageways connecting beautifully preserved homes – with stone-built furniture evocative of the people's lives: hearths, alcoves, stone box beds, even lavatories, and – perhaps most appealing – a dresser at the centre of each home, to display a story, a sort of celebration of the sacredness of daily living. The empty shelves are full of echoes of attention to little things. The dressers and the things they once displayed – bone beads, pins, pendants, paint pots, stones with designs and decorations no one knows the meaning of – are homely ... and enigmatic. Experts wonder about the meaning of these small things in much the same way as they wonder about gigantic stone circles.

When the storm first disturbed the dunes, what was revealed was a huge refuse heap – or midden – into which the village was built. Before it was excavated the midden cocooned the houses and spread over the top of the roofed passages. Long before the building of the pyramids, daily activities were carried out on its surface. It was seen as essential building material and the creation of the midden heap was the first stage in the construction process. This sweet, well-rotted compost covered walls and floors and wasn't unpleasant. It gave to homes an earthiness: a sense of home ground, common ground. As well as warming and protecting the people, midden gave them a strong sense of identity, binding them together in community, saying, 'This is our place, of us … and out there is the whole world.' I can imagine that recycling gave them a sense of the realness of themselves and enabled them to grasp the idea that other people were as real as they were. There are connections between recycling and peace.

The whole place is an earthy parable, full of ageless nuggets of truth. This was a community of people doing things in a common manner. It's an ordinary place, and yet it's extraordinary. It's a place of sharing and harmony, of recycling and peace, of compost and cupboards, which touches the mystery of being human. What has the most impact on me is that no weapons were found. All the evidence is that these ancient people had ways of resolving conflict that were peaceful. The society appears to have been egalitarian without hereditary or all-embracing leadership, although maybe it had leaders with special skills to guide folk in their different activities.

They were better at both living in community and recycling than we are! If you have never done so, try to visit Skara Brae one day. It's not a dead place but a haunting, breathing lesson in community and compost from five thousand years ago.

what i know about orkney is that …

… the story and poetry
of all experience
continually colours
my perceptions;

... the sea lapping
at life's edge
can be seen
almost everywhere

and where you can't see it
you know it's there
just over the hill;

... the isle is full of music,
wave roll, bird cry,
wind in the grass,
wind over rock,
wind made solid
by its ever-presence;

... larks and curlews
soar and sing
the whole summer night;

... sometimes silences are planted
on bare hillsides and blossom
into the wordless stories
of gardens;

... two tone weathering sandstone,
sculptured by wind and rain,
and uncanny light
make St Magnus Cathedral
a people's place,
a homecoming beyond home
in music, memory
and centring story.

a day in october

A woman smartly dressed
standing alone in a bus shelter
against a background
of obscene graffiti;
the pattern fallen leaves make
on the pavement
and the wild world
of the treetops,
above the motorway
and the John Lewis store
starlings dancing in time
to their own music.

web

(for Pat, with love)

Threads that carry moisture
drops and attach with fine touch
to feathers of grass
which then bow slightly
under the weight of gathered air.

In form, whole and almost perfect,
but not quite, for the great world
can't be perfect
but must be trusted.

We can't know the web of being,
only that we need such gentleness
only that we recognise the weight
of nothing and the risks
of touch so tender
yet strong enough
to bear for a time
the mist of thought.

A poem you said ... so I look for
something different, startling maybe
but how could I show other
than the everyday web –
delicate, enduring

and always surprising.

poet in the gallery

Simon Armitage reading
at the Pier Art Gallery, Stromness

Words settle in the space between,
wash over Shell and Pebble*,
Shellmoon* Goddess ship*;
8 Sceptres*, Fields About Me*,
First Light** and Skimmer.**

The shape of each sound
is as solid as carved wood or stone
and yet as soft as a child's hand
reaching out from far away
to touch a poet's tears.

Words carved out in the silence,
and given frail existence
live on eternally.

They touch the edge
of perception,
showing the way
to what is always
unsaid.

* Sculptures by Frances Pelly
** Sculptures by John Cumming

wild places

There is hope
beyond measure
in the way small boys
turn over dead wood
to see worms and beetles:
to know the half hidden
world of small things.

iron age camp

The bull above all, watching
kingly on his mound;
sunlight and shadows;
whispering voices in the air:
voices from the present
hardly within hearing
voices from the past,
the possibility of something
unseen – imagined
in the leaves
or rushing through the grass,
so close, almost known.

The calling buzzards
waiting their moment;
a magical light on the trees;
movement of a hare
streaking across the field.

wood

New growth from old wood
like faith revived,
or the quiet movement
of resurrection.

The forest is the soul's interior,
both rootedness and spirit unconfined,
and always the possibility
of growth, of knowing
your part in the landscape.

Always the warm glow
of wood.

watercress and harebells

– a Hertfordshire childhood

The peppery, earthy, river smell
of watercress beds that clung
to us all summer long

mingles with the memory
of warm grass and harebells
that brushed our faces
like a gentle poem as we lay
looking up at an empty sky.

Did we squander grace, I wonder,
not knowing how to honour
these times, or is the unknowing
carried within us: a place
of peace too deep for words?

against forgetting ...

Chives are indestructible.
Once planted in a garden
they stay for ever.

*

Curlew and lark
make music
in the holding dark.
Meadowsweet reflected in water
seeds the edges.

*

By the stone wall
the sheep scrape
an oval path:
a peaceful place,
innocent and holy.

*

The day, an empty bowl,
is the unit by which life
must be seized
and made whole.

I give back my life
one day at a time.

*

A lifetime getting to know
one field, one tree,
one blade of grass
one grain of sand.

postcards from iona

You will know the place,
the sweep of the bay,
the way down to the waves,
the particularity of
each path and pebble
as it waits to be chosen.

You will know the seat
where I sit to write and wonder
what each of you will feel
when the card arrives.
Will you hear
a chorus of memories?
Will you see
your child selves:
racing across the sand,
leaping waves,
loving the freedom?

Today my hands are full
of shadows and the song
the wind sang
in the nunnery ruins
is made up of fragments
of moments – earthed
in a place so lovely
that looking hurts
almost.

This is truly an isle
full of noises – its secret
whispered across the water

and in each drop of rain
as it begins to fall
on the words I write.

buckinghamshire beeches

They are the people's trees:
practical plants, of much use,
and little mystery.

Yet they offer knowledge,
bring with them a name:
'bok' or' buche' from the Norse
for 'book' or a story
written on their being
in softest charcoal.

Their image is feminine –
an elegant foil
to the masculine oak
some say.

They are socially modest, wild
in woodlands, but mostly planted
to provide wood for furniture,
rarely the rich landowners' choice.

They have a painterly beauty
and disorderly promise
that touches the heart.
So in a moment strangely sweet
a small boy stops in his tracks
to see better how the light comes

through gossamer-fringed leaves,
to touch the solid pewter trunk,
to sense the shape
of what it means
to be alive.

cow parsley

Great swathes of it
as if a dressmaker
has laid out fine lace
for a bride to be.

Paths and by-ways are edged
with its grace
and orange tips welcomed
without effort.

It benefits from our folly*
and, lighter than hemlock,
it bears us no ill.

Each airy flowerhead
is a shimmery pattern
for a story, articulate
when words run out.

*Some say cow parsley benefits from heavy use of fertilisers and overdoses of nitrogen from traffic fumes.

the smell of a book

A closed book
is like a winter wood,
deep-rooted, earthbound
with a scent of homeland.
But once its pages are open
and its words set free
it smells like the wind
in the trees,
or a summer breeze
over warm grass.

scissors

Cold to my touch,
the metal almost black
and rusted in places,
the centre bolt worn smooth:
they carry their age
with style.

There's a maker's mark
I can't quite read
but I can see 'Norwich'
where the story began,
around 1924 when my mother,
at just fourteen, began work
in a shoe factory.

They helped her cut free
from the bonds of service,
stayed with her into adult life,
possibly the only thing
she owned in her childhood,
and a reminder of the ever-present
possibility of poverty.

They were used all the years
of my childhood, their place
never taken by a new pair
and they held on to their secret
until just before she died.
Then they came to me
with their enduring story
of a changing world,
and a cutting-edge dream.

hanging out the words

A memory of Mondays:
Mum stirring up cleanliness
with a bleached stick
creating a rhythm
of hiss and flap and slop,
steam and sweat and shiny faces,
water and soap rainbows.

Then the lines: patterns
of sleeves and legs,
shorts and little dresses,
matching pants and lace-edged vests,
shirts, sheets and socks,
petticoats and pillow cases
jumpers and skirts.
They are the bunting of the days
of our working and playing,
the flags of our loyalty and loving,
the procession of our lives
hanging out to dry.
They make a story
that won't be untold:
when someone dies
the wearer's smell
doesn't wash out.

Today my washing
won't be dry by dusk.
The days are golden
but getting shorter
and slower. I am reading
between lines of clothes.
The sun is losing power.
I'm beginning to feel cold.

the colour of maybe

Yellow ochre is the painterly colour
I didn't want in my paintbox.
Not yellow enough, I thought,
for my childhood dreams.

Years later, I find it more pleasing
and feel an affinity
with its soil and sand
mellowness, an essential
for pots and the paintings
of indigenous peoples.

It's a tool-like colour
wanting to be handled –
warm enough for comfort
like the heart
of the earth itself.

st john's wort ...

... midsummer sunlike
blooms with blood red juice:
a reminder of the Baptist's death*,
a plant still burnt on some hilltops
to meet the purifying flame,
the first touch of light
on the far horizon.

All things move in wordless song
to celebrate the year's high point:
uncanny times when spirits walk
and thought wanders barefoot
in summer woods.

The imagined and the real:
a plant will heal
with punctured leaves**
and the sun will rise
because the earth turns.

*Celebrations coincided with the Feast of St John the Baptist
**St John's Wort is said to heal wounds

ringing rock – iona

There is this rock
resting on the shore
at the North End
of the island.
It's lichen-covered
and the wind rushes over it
silently. But take a stone,
tap the rock
and there's music
in the air.

I imagine taking them all –
William, Alasdair, Emily and Oliver* –
along the shore to this place
to touch the orange lichen,
feel the wind ruffle their hair,
smell the salt of the sea
but above all

to take in the ring
of this magical rock,

this piece of the earth
of which we are made.

I think they would understand
and treasure forever
the life of a sound
that exists for a moment
so always has being
like the wind that carries it
far out over the sea.

* My grandchildren

tea with mr and mrs pillinger

They were almost strangers.
Not quite, she became my Godmother.
Mum treated them with diffidence.
They were middle class – posh even –
but displaced by war.
They had money
and bought a security
we never thought about.
We lived in the same house for years
and never used their first names.
We didn't often go into 'their' room,
the best room in our house.

One day we did.
I followed mum
and saw first the shine
on the top of the sideboard
all the way along one wall.
It looked slippery, wet almost.
Then, on top, just within my sight,
like the floating water lilies
I'd seen on a pond in the park,
oh joy, cakes, with icing
and when I put up my hand
I could just reach ...

winter haiku

Windblown summer chairs,
stacked like rhyming poems, wait
for the returning sun.

Bare trees blow and bend
dark-limbed in silent greeting,
The air is songless.

One woman walking
on the empty road
towards the city.

what i know about orchards ...

... is that they test the seasons,
flaunting blossom,
feeding wild things.

I may be comforted
by little ordered groves
neither field
nor woodland,
neither place to hunt
nor place to gather
but place to be.

There are voices in the trees
and you can hear apples fall
long after the trees stop fruiting.

mythweaver

Gnarled, bent and far away
from the trees of the forest
it flaunts the pink and white
apple blossom innocence
of half-remembered youth
and forgotten lovers.

One alone, paradise behind a fence,
colonised by lichen, touched by time
and the scent of garden roses,
a stranger to sweeten the streets
with dreams of rainlight
on morning apples.

mellow fruitfulness

Cherries as ripe as memories
of the lips of love,
damsons that blush purple
in the sun, push deep red
against the jam jar,
apples lost in long grass,
the essence of stillness,
waiting for all our tomorrows;
or growing red against a wall
taking the colour as quietly
as the penetrating light,
or little apples –
Beauty of Bath maybe –
that, fresh from the tree,
fit a child's hand
and tingle on the tongue
of memory.

In spring, I might be comforted
by the promise of trees in bloom
and the memory of abundant fruiting.

beauty of bath

A vigorous tree, the experts say,
with easily damaged fruit
suited to a gentle garden.
Never much of an orchard apple.

In early childhood
I saw it first
through a broken fence:
a tree covered with little apples
that hung like Christmas baubles.
I came to love these pretty fruits
with their red-flushed, mottled skin,
leaking pink into soft white flesh.

You could see it in the face:
that tingly taste on the tongue:
the first bite of fading summer
from a fruit that wants to be eaten
straight from the tree, a beauty
that won't grow old with grace
but must be enjoyed
now.

the boat

Begin with the boat,
a thing so small,
thirsty and waiting.
Sun sets on its worn wood.
The possibility of moonlight
floods its gaps.

Whether there is too much
or too little boat depends
on the depths
of my imagination.

Not the splash of the oars
nor the turn of the tiller
but dolphins, gannets
and the magic
a child sees
in the bow wave
will guide me far enough out
to lay the oars on my knees,

to wait, filled with the rowan tree
and the hope of walking a field
on another shore, wait alone
in the no-looking-back quiet
for a whisper of wind
to blow the boat far off.

part two

seeing

a grain of sand

In the intricate dance
of earth, air, fire, water
a grain of sand,
waiting on life.

A lifted, moving, making
grain, carrying unseen,
for the whole world,
a burden of microbes

from Sahara desert,
to Amazon rainforest.

Billions of nutrients,
from poor to rich

to encourage seeding,
to promise growth.

How great the beauty
of this interdependence.
Without deserts, no forests:
a speck of thought
that can never again
be too small to matter.

Notes:

Sometime between 1801 and 1805 William Blake wrote, in *Auguries of Innocence*:

> To see a World in a Grain of Sand
> And a Heaven in a Wild Flower,
> Hold Infinity in the palm of your hand
> And Eternity in an hour.

In 2010 scientists discovered that for thousands of years nutrients have been carried on Saharan dust to the rainforests of the Amazon.

seeing

So poetry is something fine within us. It is how we see the thing itself. It's hope, creativity, celebration and joy. It's surprise but above all it's love and beauty: the beauty of the moment, the understanding, the connections.

The poet Thomas Hardy wanted to be remembered as someone who noticed things: small things like hedgehogs travelling 'furtively over the lawn' and the way 'May month flaps its glad green leaves like wings' (from *Afterwards*). He more than 'noticed'. He attended closely to littleness, seeing with a poetic eye. This is about retaining our sense of wonder so that in spite of everything else – the sorrows and horrors, the speed and the noise, the crowds and the busyness – we still notice and can rejoice in the small events of our living.

Experiences to which we give our full and compassionate attention are understood differently, seen with an ongoing awareness of the wonder of life itself that lifts our whole being. In a sense, we are singing the creation – the details, the particulars and the whole: the way the features of a room take on a significance as we wait for a birth, sit with a sick child, or watch with the dying. We are not praying exactly but our consciousness is heightened and we notice, somehow differently, what's in the room: the curtains, the carpet, the pictures on the walls. The landscape of our lives is made up of such moments and such particulars. There is that which gives us life and that which gives us love of life, which is visionary and has power to transform the way we see the world. Seeing connections, paying attention … that's what matters, that's the beauty. The heightened awareness in Hardy's poems seems always to be against a background of remembered love, the remembered beautiful moment.

Why does the experience of beauty produce such strong

sensations in humans? The question, like so many important questions, has no answer but to wonder at life lived amongst the joys and sorrows of ordinary existence. Beauty is unquantifiable. It can't be counted or measured, bought or sold. It's the sanctity and preciousness of life. Beauty is forgiveness, delight, love, respect, wisdom, awe, wonder, truth, purity, justice, courage, fun, compassion, challenge, knowledge, trust. Remove any one of these values from our communities and our quality of life, the way we engage in relationships, would be radically changed. These are what make our everyday experiences sacred.

My book *Words and Wonderings* includes a conversation with Satish Kumar (Editor of *Resurgence* magazine) in which he talks of beauty as central to his teachings, as food for the soul. Beauty, he says, is 'the window through which we can reach out for a balanced, socially just, ecologically sustainable, spiritually fulfilling lifestyle.' Simplicity is essential, as are humility and attentiveness – seeing things as they are and for what they are. The author Adam Nicolson, in his book *The Smell of Summer Grass*, tells of his joy in his hayfield which he manages to support a diversity of flowers. His neighbour tells him, 'It's a desert … It'd hardly be worth baling … It's all top and no bottom.' It clearly had no value … and yet it is beautiful, and to be beautiful is also a form of value and matters to us … matters to the richness of our being alive.

We need to be able to see and discern for ourselves, to make beauty necessary. What we see may be valued *because* we make it the subject of poetry/theology, the subject of our wonder and celebration. Things also take on significance because they are the subject of our questions, particularly the big questions: What makes fullness of life and ethical living? And why is it often almost impossible today? Are we prepared to speak the wrong?

Of course, the poetry of our lives is also about outrage, dread, horror and fear – life at its most raw and unprotected (see 'Skeleton Tree', page 89). That huge 'Why?' that we hold deep inside us isn't an intellectual question. It's a cry of agony and the poetry of tears.

We need poetry to remind us of the riches in diversity, in the untidy details of life, and the love, fear, remorse, wonder, pity of it. This is where hope lies. The resurrection moment will come from this place. The vision will come from the things *you* see and know, out of the messy details of your life, your experience. Poetry is the art of imagining: seeing things wholly as they are and seeing something different. It's love that makes the imaginary real. It's love that makes necessity beautiful.

When Nicodemus came to Jesus for rules, for a plan, Jesus saw poetry. When Mary poured out the precious oil, the disciples cried 'Waste!' and Jesus saw beauty.

the path

We are on a path
of blessing or curse:

humanity,

old, run wild, a species
with talk, ancient talk

to illumine each moment
for always.

We watch the memory
carried in child after child
of the dawn, the beginning.

what i know about flowers ...

is a tenderness of colours
that makes my heart leap.

They lead me to an understanding
beyond their names and details.

Placed in a vase by a window
they make one revealing surprise
of the very near and the very far,
the tangible and the intangible,
the small and the vast,

and the merest suggestion
of that middle distance
which my eyes leap over.

There is something humbling
about the intensity of blue
in the details of a bluebell
or the vastness of the sky,
the concentration of yellow:
a buttercup in full flower
or the beam of the sun.

If you don't feel
the colour and the light
the looking becomes nothing.

The painterly joy of colour revealed
by one who knows quiet flowers,
butterwort or bogbean,
dusky cranesbill or daffodils,
might light a room

no beginning, no ending
just awakening.

waiting

They also serve who only stand and wait – familiar words from one of the sonnets of poet John Milton, *When I consider how my light is spent*, written in 1673 when he became blind.

There isn't anything glamorous or romantic about waiting and yet it is, as Milton noted, an activity of some significance. We are all too aware of refugees huddled at borders, waiting to move on; people seeking asylum detained, waiting for officialdom to do its job; queues for this or that item of food, a weekly waiting routine for so many; children with bowls and hungry faces, waiting for food. All who, like Hagar in the Bible story, wait on the margins of our society. If you have no money, no home, nowhere to go, you'll know all about waiting.

But waiting often embodies a quietness that is charged with hope and attentiveness, which is the rarest and purest form of generosity – a just and loving gaze on all that is.

Waiting closes the gap between being and doing in a way which women (but of course not only women) have always known: waiting for the birth of a baby, waiting at the bedside of a sick child, grandmothers waiting for bread, waiting with the dying, waiting for news of someone missing. A fresco by Fra Angelico in one of the cells of the monastery of San Marco in Florence bears witness to a beautiful legend that while the apostles slept in the Garden of Gethsemane even though Jesus had asked them to stay awake and pray, two women, Mary and Martha, were watching and waiting at the gates of the garden.

People can be a presence and a protest as they wait, expressing the quiet beauty of compassion, of waiting upon life, and acting as a tangible sign of our vision of a more just, peaceful, loving world. In that tangibility is the hope that such a world might become a reality. The Women in Black international network is one example. They resist all forms of violence and build bridges across differences and borders based on a shared perspective which they create as they wait at regular times, silently, non-violently, in public places. They carry placards, hand out leaflets and wear black to signify mourning for those who have died as a result of war and violence. They bear witness.

As Mary bears witness. Mary sings *Magnificat*, a song of liberation, not just for the sake of being heard but for the sake of a better world. *Magnificat* – sung by a pregnant woman, a waiting song.

At the time of the terror in Russia, during the 1930s and '40s, Russian poet Anna Ahkmatova, even when ill, would get up from bed to go and stand, sometimes in freezing weather, in the long lines of people waiting outside the prisons. She hoped to be able to see her son who had been arrested for little other reason than that he had her, a subversive poet, as a mother. Once as she stood in the queue another woman asked her if she could put this into words. She did – in the form of a poem she called *Requiem* in which Mary the mother of Jesus, at his crucifixion, stands apart, watching him: 'No other looked/into her secret eyes. Nobody dared.'

And so a poet takes the suffering of all mothers to the silent place where Mary of the Magnificat waits at the foot of the cross.

a very poetic prophet

John the Baptist – now there's someone worth thinking about. He's always been a favourite of mine, a big, surprising character appearing out of the desert still wearing his camel-hair coat and probably carrying a lunchbox of locusts. There's something poetic about John. He's wonderfully off-centre – a challenge to the relentless roll of reason and logic. He is unkempt, angry, unbending … and larger than life.

His cries are loud and insistent: 'Wake up! See the light! Repent!' – a wilderness voice crying out in love and longing where he sees poverty, loneliness, suffering, hunger, homelessness, oppression, marginalisation; saying things could be different, preparing the way for change.

Many would say he is naïve, or simply doesn't understand the complexities of the situation. But his simple message puts the fear of God into the oppressors, the powerful, the men in suits! *He isn't asking for restructuring or adjustments in programmes.* He's calling for a complete change of heart so that all may share in the earth's good gifts. Share, deal honestly, don't bully or oppress, 'prove' your repentance – a message that holds good today.

John's vision is of a just society where people share, and care for one another, where peace isn't the quiet of fear but the babble of freedom. Like so many outspoken characters before and after him, he ends up in prison and is eventually put to death.

Many people imprisoned for protesting about the wrongs in society are poets, which isn't as surprising as it might at first seem. Even the simplest poem may open up imaginative possibilities, stir your emotions and seriously affect the way you see, the way you feel. That's why I see John as a poetic character – he touches hearts. He asks people to feel sorry for what is wrong – to hope – and to imagine lives and communities transformed.

Imagination matters. Imagining a better world, telling of mystery and wonder, joy and pain, hopes and visions is threatening to those who cannot see beyond facts, policies, statistics, programmes or market forces. Poets persuade us to dream, to think of alternatives, to look for another way ... to surprise ourselves.

John is angry. He sees the need for big changes. He also carries and encourages a huge sense of expectation, of undying hope. Something *good* is coming. His sanger is an essential prelude to the coming joy, the new wholeness, the better world waiting to be born.

through a glass darkly ...

Greenhouses, the almost summer
smell of tomatoes and the sounds
of breaking glass beckon the ghosts
of her lost dreams.

He spent hours reclaiming glass
but it was never bright and clear
as she wanted glass to be.

From outside he was just visible
among the plants. The tomatoes,
he said, would taste the sweetest ever
but they never did.

a seasoned day ...

tasty,
salt on the wind
but the sea far off.

Waves of silver and gold
sea buckthorn part
to let us pass
into a jewelled light
where words go missing.

'what makes a person holy?'

Outside of board rooms and conferences, I don't much like resolutions – the sort of thing you might think of at New Year, based on illusory certainties, on an understanding of life as some sort of seventy-year business plan …

Life isn't like that. It's wonder, mystery … and uncertainty. People are muddled, mixed-up creatures. None of this lends itself to the making of resolutions. We are born, we die – that's certain – but in between there isn't a line from a to b. It's a cycle of seasons, celebrations and mournings, work and leisure, eating and sleeping, beginnings and endings.

Within the cycle are many threshold moments. I think of a favourite picture of mine, Winifred Nicholson's *The Gate to the Isles*. The gate is an exquisite blue; through the gate is a sea-filled morning place … space, distance … and the possibility of islands …

I like the promise of such threshold places: gates, doors, bridges, arches and rainbows; times when we stand at the gate: of adulthood, of a new relationship, of life or the end of life. We celebrate and mourn these times, mark them with ritual and story, share them with family, friends and community who will support us into the unknown.

So, at the gate of the years, closing and opening, we have parties and fun; maybe we reflect a bit and become open to the unknown future. We look back on the sadness and the blessings of the year that is dying but try not to hang on to it too tightly. The threshold is a vulnerable place – a place of surrendering and letting go.

We look forward without grasping at certainty. For what is certainty but wanting to master what can't be known. Let us live humbly and compassionately with uncertainty and confusion, accepting both the wonder and the accompanying risks, and being ready for new impressions and opportunities.

New Year partying comes naturally out of the celebrations of the birth of a baby at Christmas. Mary, the mother of Jesus, sings her song, the *Magnificat* – heard in churches all over the world at Christmas – from a threshold. She sings to the unborn child, not knowing what the future will be for either of them. She sings a song of freedom and solidarity. It is also, when juxtaposed with images of human suffering, a song of outrage. We need songs like this. They give us the energy to trust the unknown future. Mary sings, and after the birth of Jesus, when the strange visitors – shepherds and wise men – have left, she doesn't make resolutions or prepare mission statements. She ponders things in her heart.

The Buddha was once asked, 'What makes a person holy?' He replied, 'Every hour is divided into a certain number of seconds and every second into a certain number of fractions. Anyone who is able to be totally present in each fraction of a second is holy.' There is nothing common about common life – it takes an awakened sense to see what is mysterious in each ordinary moment, to ponder in our hearts, to really see people and things – not our preconceptions of them.

So, on the threshold where past and future meet in the present, let's look slowly and listen to the heartbeat of life, guided by love with justice and by whatever makes our whole being sing. Let us step out into the uncertainty, celebrating, trusting and open to each precious moment.

In the soft light this evening
I sense the approaching winter.
The nights will be different now
with cold and candles
to be snuffed out
carefully.

surprise!

Strawberries may be available all year now but isn't that first bite into the flesh of a freshly picked strawberry at the beginning of summer still a surprise? The colour, the smell, the juice over your tongue ... and the flavour. It's meadow flowers, summer breezes and the freedom of childhood. It's the taste of love and memory, of the hopes and dreams of a land flowing with milk and honey. In Cherokee native American homes strawberries are often kept to remind people not to argue. They are a symbol of good luck.

Giving full attention to this familiar fruit – picked from our gardens and fields, bought in the supermarket, on roadside stalls – is an awakening when we see for a moment that there is nothing mundane about strawberries, nothing common about the common life, nothing ordinary about ordinary things.

Strawberries grasp all our senses. Look at them. Have you ever seen such glowing red? It's passion and it's joy – a colour like the sound of a trumpet. Part of the created world seems to cry out: 'Don't you see the wonder?' Has familiarity made us stop wondering at the beauty of this astonishing fruit? Suppose strawberries were new. Suppose they had just come into the world and we had not seen them before. Imagine our delight. Imagine what the very first taste, the first one ever, would be like – how astonishing, how enchanting, how *surprising*.

Surprise is at the heart of the world we think we know, a world more extraordinary than we realise. It may be a cliché but life *is* full of surprises! – imaginative moments of awakening when tiny gestures, like a baby's outstretched hands, small things like stones, spoons, flowers seem to amaze us as never before ... with their wonder, mystery and value ... when a grasshopper is as exciting as a dragon ... and a strawberry as fresh and new as if we were eating it in Eden.

It's all about how you see. Seamus Heaney, in his lovely poem *At the Wellhead*, tells of a blind neighbour, Rosie Keenan, 'Who played the piano all day in her bedroom':

> *... Being with her*
> *was intimate and helpful, like a cure*
> *you didn't notice happening. When I read*
> *a poem with Keenan's well in it, she said,*
> *'I can see the sky at the bottom of it now.'**

That's surprise! And poetry. A blind woman seeing the sky at the bottom of a well. It can't be explained. We don't make sense of these moments. They just happen. We see clearly and we want to sing for joy – or sorrow – to write, paint, take photographs, for these surprising insights are creative.

The seventeenth-century poet Thomas Traherne wrote: *Your enjoyment of the world is never right till every morning you awake in Heaven ... till the Sea itself flows in your veins, till you are clothed with the heavens, and crowned with the stars.* He knew that surprise is about seeing with our whole being, not just our eyes, and about living every moment fully. We don't know where it's coming from, this huge surprise of life. The point is not to know but to live and to love.

* From 'At the Wellhead', included in *The Spirit Level*, Seamus Heaney, Faber, London 1996

after lunch

(10th June 2011, for Lesley)

After you had left, I wandered
in the fields, watching
butterflies and wondered
about beauty, words,
food and fantasies:

the way one word
stimulates another,
the way images
and ideas intermingle;

our love of things
and the way this creates

the music of conversation
and the conversation of music;

space, books and good bread.

Somewhere in there
is the vital ingredient
but there's no need
to know what it is

just that it's there
and that it makes life
good.

walking to erraid

across the almost dry sea bed
we are like drowned people
moved by the tides. Seabed smells
rise around us, letting out secrets.
We touch the intimacy of places,
stories revealed in sand ripples, suggesting
soft ambiguous forms, remembered
or half suspected, waiting for the sighs
of the sea coming back, slipping
through imagination and memory
like music, or colour,
wordless.

butterfly

(For Andrew, with love)

The light in your eyes
said all we could hope to say.
Unknowing, you let go
the colours of creation,
a beauty you couldn't hold
but released to be part of you.
The butterfly promise
endured through the years
of your growing
and the light shines on
undiminished.

a memory of apples

Gnarled branches, knot and hook,
limb on limb, lichen covered,
sparse in their winter grace,
the old trees are weary
with blossoming.

Shadowy ladders and laden baskets,
the air heady with apple scents
and the sounds of harvest
– all memory, or maybe dream.
Now a quiet fruiting offers food
for birds and butterflies, mostly.
Occasionally, you might see
a Camberwell Beauty*
feeding on fallen plums.
But the Black Veined White
last fed among fruit trees
in the 1920s and is no more

in this place of dappled stories
where the humble wild apple,
mother of many varieties
still lingers at the edges,
holding on.

*Seen near Prestwood, Bucks, in 2006.
First time in this country since 1995

pomona and vertumnus*

The ground beneath the trees
awaits her silent tread
as she comes to meet
her ever changing lover.
Fallen apples, the essence
of stillness, hide in the grass.
Dead wood and twisted branches
make strange shapes, familiar
yet unknown.

There are owls here
and dogs bark at night
in the distance. Deer linger
in the undergrowth.
Stag beetles rely on dead wood
to survive.

Light penetrates the trees
to swell the fruit and colour it
quietly. Apples flush
with their own variety,
relishing difference.
Cherries glow red
as the lips of love.
Damsons, modest fruit,
blush purple in the sun
and later glow
deep burgundy,
preserved

like the bitter sweet
taste of her dreams.

s

*From Ovid's *Metamorphoses*. Pomona is a wood nymph, goddess of fruit trees; Vertumnus the god of changing seasons and ripening autumn fruits. He has the power to change his shape (and became associated with money changing) and falls in love with Pomona. He follows her around as a harvester, herdsman or vinedresser and in the form of an old woman begs Pomona to have pity on him. He succeeds only when he reverts to his true shape.

re-shaping

Espalier, cordon, fan
trees shaped
like Pomona's cloak,
like angel wings.

Young limbs pushed out
and held against the warmth
of the wall, holding the light,
growing brick-coloured
apples.

after the war

Steamy air is heavy
with the smell of baby soap;
small hands reach out for bubbles,
and burst rainbows.

Bootsteps sound on the stairs;
the door frame fills with khaki.

He has come early,
holds only the tin
painted as a wrapped parcel,
lines like Christmas ribbons.

He opens it. She is entranced
by lollipops, sugared jellies,
dolly mixtures, barley sugar,
allsorts.

The unforgettable colours
of sweets from a stranger.

brave new morning

Heady with the satisfactions
of home: the smells
of newly baked bread
and wind-dried sheets
folded in the sun,

I have come
to a desolation
of stained concrete
and the smell
of despair.

No one is here.
No hand is raised
for 'spare change'.
No eyes look up to pierce
my affluent self-satisfaction
or say what it is possible to say
silently with unwashed flesh.

I am passing cleanly by
on the other side
of an empty space
and breathing in
the pungent scent
of homelessness.

come yew hare long o me

(For my mother)

A movement of the wrist
that's all it seems to the child
watching, and the bones are out.

She could gut and fillet
a herring as deftly
as any fishwife

yet her voice was soft.
with the Norfolk lilt
of a Norwich girl
who rolled sounds together
like waves on the shore.

Child of the home counties,
I grew up with a sense
of that distant sea
and her names for things:
dodderman, bishy barny bee,
answered her invitation:
'Come yew hare long o me'

to the sweet poetry
of her place
never my home
but in my blood.

She told me
'You're thur one to spearke well' –
but hers was the true voice,
the one with sounds
as basic as gutting fish,
the one that said
'Belonging'.

the moment's song

That morning seemed to be outside time.
The cool darkness of an almost empty church
mingled with the blown scents
of grass and meadow flowers.

I looked up and saw your face
framed by the window leaded
with sunlit trees,
the light solid on every leaf,
echoing a silence more ancient
than any history, any carved word
caught in air, or stone remembrance;
a silence I would remember
as an expression of pure joy
close to ecstasy.

sweet sorrow

The path from you
to me suffers little
from lack of use.
I could walk there today
and know the strangeness
would be nothing more
than a few dead leaves
blown along the way.

self portrait

Watcher in the mirror
I follow you
wide-eyed and pondering
youth and age
time present
and time past.

I look into the fire
of those eyes
nearly seventy years old
as they follow me
and ask:
What do you see?
What reflection of a life
is there in the painterly eyes?
Is it a reflection of my self
or me looking and experiencing
you?

what i know about war ...

Between my finger and my thumb
The squat pen rests.
I'll dig with it
Seamus Heaney *

What I know about war
comes out in the night
in a mindless scream

for something forgotten
but written on the body

and suppressed at the sight
on screen or in photographs
of children's hands reaching out
from their terror
to my hidden knowing.

*

There may be words
for this way of knowing
the shape, the movement
the over and over roundness
and presence of words
pushing letter by letter
at the edge of my thought.

*

I dig with the pen
and so write the fear,
write the noise,
uncover the meanings
of hope
and move words out
of futility
towards an ever-retreating
silence.

* From 'Digging' included in *Death of a Naturalist*, Faber, 1966

war

This memory is without
words or understanding,
being before I knew language.
It's a deeply buried fear
sometimes stirred by the sounds
of ordinary life:
grinds and bangs,
rumbles and crashes,
fireworks and thunderstorms,
sirens and whistles;
pneumatic drills and vacuum cleaners
aircraft and strimmers,
or even the anticipation
of these things.
Noise lodges in my flesh
like a lifelong scar
from an act of violence.

demolition

Jagged cement blocks, stones,
twisted wire, crumpled metal,
three stately chairs, like old men
hanging on in dusty splendour
for a party that won't happen,
broken china, an upturned cot,
shelves and a few books
dealing words to the wind.

A place someone came to know
as home, a sacred space,
diminished to a rubble pile,
yet still it holds the voices
of the people who lived there

and the stones will always tell
what has been. They shout aloud
when the bulldozers come
and we are silent.

Home violated,
inner things laid bare
and somewhere far away
a stranger weeps.

pearls

(after reading *Eyes in Gaza**)

Some people say that pearls are tears.
I have never liked pearls
and yet at this moment
of total helplessness
could I wear a string of pearls
against my heart
to weep for Gaza's children?

* *Eyes in Gaza* by Mads Gilbert and Erik Fosse, published by Quartet Books Ltd, 2010

it's a question

of trust in vulnerability.

Know that in the exposure
of whitish green flesh
your 'empire' is doomed,
your power a fantasy.

Unclothed you are no more
than the next small scrap
of suffering humanity

kicking on straw.

skeleton tree

Stripped to something beyond
itself, hint of bone,
bleached white
yet somehow undead,
proud against the sky,
absorbing the sound
of the sea.

Salt-blessed, sun-warmed
wind-worried, only half forgotten;
statuesque, a monument
to essential tree
brought to unlife
not giving way
marking a place
from which to see
the unsheltered world.

string trio, peter maxwell davies

Monday 23rd June 2008

The quickness of a reel
gently woven through a slow air.
Harmonies moving into places
where they don't usually go

and meeting with presences
comfortable and profound
in their power to discomfort.

Afterwards all thoughtfulness
turns to the remains
of pure sound

and the rhythm of muscles
the movement of line

that is a composer's smile
reaching beyond a cathedral
full of voices to the depths
of silence.

what music does

(for Emma)

Today a cellist came.
She made music
in the spare bedroom
and the space became warm
with created sounds:
a range of voice
from tears to laughter,
from youth to age
all the living and loving
that this old house
may, or may not,
have known.

They'll stay – these notes –
the way sounds of trees falling
are there when nobody hears,
or a cuckoo's call
is heard in winter,
or birds and butterflies
are unseen but known
in quiet movement of air

and the house will never
be the same.

iona morning

A painterly prospect.
Light on things:
the way the rising sun
touches smallness: a fusion
of flowers, unidentified;
the wood of the compost bin
looking as if a moment ago
someone left in a hurry
leaving a task unfinished.

Far off against the sea the ruins of a room,
nearer the beginning or end of a wall.
There will always be fragmentary walls

as we might think there will always be
the Abbey. The same light touches
all and I stand waiting in the cool dew
of a morning that is now, for always
and could be the beginning of time.

winding ways and accidental flowers

There's the journey
and the end
of the journey
which is not a destination;
there's the sound of a human voice
bringing hope in the emptiness;

there's the way the sun
touches trees and grass
of a summer evening;
there's the smell of the grass
when it's warm;

there's the way the bread
uses the touch
of human hands

and a child's feet
feel the earth
as she takes her first steps;

there's a drop of rain
on lady's mantle leaves
and the way a child notices;

there's the path into the poetry
of silence and uncertainty,
the gaps and spaces
through the words

and the way I know.

holding on

Know what hand pushes
the boat out, the scent
of a shadow on worn wood –
something or nothing
gently perceived.
As an old violin
retains its voice
when played by others,
so a boat unmoored at dawn
drifts like a half-forgotten dream
between green islands.

There is comfort in the shape,
the cradling image that holds meaning
and beauty too, as in all things
where need determines shape
and you have use of the vessel.

part three

sharing

all the earth

A precious story from the past,
a mystery for all our futures.

A subtle wisdom
growing at the pace
of nature itself,
not too fast,
not taking too much.

Seeds are truthful
to their own place

and saving them is sacred duty.
Be careful where you keep
these originators of life.
They need beautiful storage:
clay pots of many colours
or maybe bamboo baskets
places of worship, altars,
places of wonder.

Painstaking preservation,
local varieties, indigenous stories,
the seeds' story is bounty and generosity,
to be shared, borrowed,
exchanged, never traded.
A sort of revolution.
A way of knowing.

sharing

Looking and seeing, the radiance of things, the poetic view, heightened awareness and consciousness. Then comes the need to tell, to express, what we have seen and experienced, to share in relationship with others our joy, sorrow, despair, remorse. This is something of what it means to be human. We 'paint' the journey, colour our living. It's much more about connections than meaning or purpose. Always we are moving towards unknowing, silence, the beautiful emptiness.

There is consolation and a great sense of peace in acknowledging our uncertainty, in not needing to *know* but being open to and trusting life. That's the creative act of love. Some might call it faith. It's where we find the strength to hope. It's where we are free. The ordinary people, the small things that touch our lives daily, are elevated when the mind is open. They are the tiny seeds from which transformation begins. The small world and the epic world are one. We are beyond the destructive questions: *Is what I'm telling, writing about, important enough? Does my experience matter?* The small and private perspective can often make, in undertones rather than tone, the most significant political or religious poem or story. The world is filled with challenges, crises, pain, disappointment – you know because you, in joy and laughter, sorrow and tears, despair and hope, have experienced them.

We need courage to share things and feelings precious to us and significant to our daily life – and that includes, of course, the values we live by. And we need compassion in listening to the stories, the experiences, of others. Often what separates and isolates us is the idea that a special language (a language of poetry or of faith?) is necessary. But we tell of life and living in the language we use every day: as simple as 'Come, and have breakfast' (page 121). Trusting and being true to *our own experiences* – that's what matters. Having the wisdom, at the appropriate time, to say 'I don't know' and to love the silence and value the unknowing.

Perhaps we need to find new ways to gather together as human beings to honour life, to worship. New ways that respect the past and tradition but don't bow to its worst aspects or silence my experience, your experience. New ways that show openness to *all that is* and *all that happens* and *all that could be,* that use discernment and intellectual discipline alongside imagination. New ways where we are not tempted to fill much needed space with inappropriate imagery, where we create a safe place within which if you can't believe something then you don't. Having faith isn't about believing impossible things. There are miracles and wonders we *can believe* every day of our lives, all around us. Faith is learning to see … and trusting our ears and eyes, our fingertips and feet, *and* our minds.

Free from absolute and supernatural claims, free from destructive, harmful dogma, free from the unbelievables with which many have struggled for years, but true to poetry and story, we can maybe celebrate all of life's moments fully and wholly and be open to words of exploration, lament and celebration that all can share. We can be open to the concerns of the world and deliver a clear message of reverence for the earth, justice, compassion, sustainable living, love of beauty, simplicity in living.

It's possibly becoming clear that I also want to question the concept of God as traditionally understood, as the focus of worship. The question is there and it won't go away but that's not what we're about at the moment. With or without the use of the word 'God', or with an openly recognised myriad different approaches, images and understandings of what we mean when we use that word, we can move to an open place with a language of connection, shared values and shared humanity – a gathering, a sacred place or space of wonder and celebration, where we understand and express what makes our hearts sing; a place of remorse, regret, lament where we understand and express what makes our hearts weep.

Poets and poetry help us imagine peace, goodness, justice, love when all we can see is disaster. Imagine, think, dream – look at what is in front of you, see that it is good and celebrate it; sing the creation! Look at what is in front of you and see the suffering and the horror and also see how it might be transformed, how you might tell it differently. *Imagine*: the abolition of slavery began when someone imagined hands without manacles. Tell the remorse, the sadness, the regret and lament. Tell the healing story and live it out. We *know* it's imagination but a different kind of knowing tells us it's also real … because it is love and justice.

To return to what I said in Beginnings, isn't this what worship really means, finding a place to express this human experience – stories not creeds, poetry not polemic? Theology after all *is* poetry.

Tell your story and from somewhere music … and poetry … emerges. The Estonian poet Jaan Kaplinski has said that his poems often aren't poems. 'They're parts of a long declaration of love to the world, a poetic list of people and things I love.'*

There are huge risks involved in this transformative, reconnected, creative-at-the-roots activity that brings into being what previously did not exist but, although the world may be bleak or terrible, it's also full of promise. Love that comes out of nothing is the great creative act, the great outpouring, in painting, music, sculpture, gardening, cooking, loving, story, and songs for celebrating, songs for lamenting, songs for awakening. Singing, at its best, has been described as a handful of birdsong and a small cup of light. I like that! Singing in its widest possible sense: not outdated theology in badly written hymns but wonder, joy, remorse, lament, all that we've explored so far, and more: singing the creation.

There is no conclusion to move towards. Poetry moves towards the only thing I want to say that glitters out of reach, the only words worth listening to that are probably the ones I can't speak … and is silent …. and no less real for being inexpressible.

I hope some of the pieces in this book will enable you to find the words to explore the poetry of your own uncertainty, to push against enclosing walls, to move around the brackets, open your thoughts to the skies … and know the peace and beauty of silence.

* From *Summers and Springs*, 1995/2004, Bloodaxe Northumberland,

brackets

I have a fondness for brackets,
for the way they enclose
the free space of imagined adventure;
for the way the inside words
leave behind the outside words
and faith is placed
in the indefinable.

prayer (1)

Stones and bones,
the sun and the moon,
wood and water
and warm wet soil.

Writing the light,
holding the light,
gathering in the last moments
the left over light.

Finding the poetry
and the stories:
mindful of cyclamen
and beech trees,
mindful of cyclamen
and olive trees;
blowing snow and the smell
of baking bread;
anemones in cracks
in rocks, and in a bucket
in a shop;
sheep and sounds and wool feel.

Mindful of humanity
and other places
other ways of being.

sacrum – the bowl of birth

The first churches: enclosed space
with windows wide open
to new winds and fresh air
from across the town
the streets, the fields
the seas, the oceans.

A place to watch
from the edges, maybe,
as monks once watched
in the stone upon stone silence
of beehive huts, to pour out sadness
sorrow, brokenness
into the unseen emptiness.

A place to weep
for the world's pain
a place to reveal the hint
of a smile, to laugh
for the world's joy.

Like an empty bowl,
a place to seek offering,
its value being breathing space
and awaited thought
or vessel implying movement.

With simple shifts of perception
we can find the sacred, small miracles
enough for the day and loaves and fishes
to pass around, share and eat.

I remember a photograph
from Kochi, South India
fisherman, wife
and child (asleep) safe
in the bowl of his round boat.

(The Japanese name for a begging bowl
is 'oryoke' – 'just enough'.)

open eyes; open hands ...

'What *is* prayer?' is a question not often asked outright. But perhaps it needs to be, not because there is an answer – there isn't – but because speaking the questions often broadens concepts and makes them more inclusive. So no answers. Just a few thoughts and more questions.

Prayer might disturb and discomfort, but can it be prayer if it bores, excludes and embarrasses? Have you ever sat listening to an extensive one-way chat with Jesus and squirmed in your seat or felt patronised and belittled when someone says, in that special voice kept for such words, 'I'll pray for you'? Why do we allow fundamentalists to get away with so much that is not only embarrassing but also dull and exclusive?

I have heard prayer described as *interactive dialogue with the world.* Interesting jargon. Isn't that mindfulness? I like that! Mindfulness is being wholly immersed in a situation, identifying fully with people, emotionally involved. Nothing boring or embarrassing in that.

As most poets realise, prayer is a thought–imagination journey of discovery and exploration. The concept is diverse, open, imaginative and exciting. And prayer has to be about openness, awareness, really seeing, paying attention to the world around us. It is nothing to do with hands together, eyes closed!

So, leave aside the baggage of creeds and dogmas, learn to be at ease with uncertainty, liberate your imagination, be totally present in the moment and place where you are, enter into the realm of poetry and art, and all sorts of things happen.

Clearly, prayer is *active;* it's about thinking, caring, connecting – as expressed by, for example, the lighting of a candle. Praying might be a way of using images, shapes and colours, threads and knots, twists and loops and symbols (like candles) to touch the springs of imagination. But prayer is more than *doing*. It's also about *being*: a state of body and mind. In Celtic spirituality praying has always been associated with the whole of life, all the time, not just at specific, set-aside moments. It's both a way of being and a way of believing the future into being. Prayer is learning to wait without fear of silence or uncertainty; so it's also about growing into maturity, ripening. Thomas Merton called it a 'discovering faculty' – like a pilgrimage – which you can use to find out about standing in your own space, about the still point of your being, about where you are most truly you. Finding yourself and experiencing connectedness with the world around you and the people in it – that's what some people might call prayer.

Serious looking has a healing beauty. Paying attention to the most minute things – stones, spoons, flowers, tiny gestures – is the most generous of human activities. It turns dead, inattentive time into living time: every moment lived fully and compassionately. In loving attention we discover the enabling grace that tunes us in to the heart-rending harmony of all creation – and that has to be prayer.

Then there is thankfulness. A constant attitude of gratitude is life-giving. Open heart and mind, enjoy the earth's good gifts and be thankful ... and know that joy in something or someone is prayer. Conversely, there is that huge 'Why?' we hold deep inside us and spit out occasionally when faced with suffering, oppression and cruelty. It isn't an intellectual question. It's a prayer.

And surprise – moments of awakening when something small and ordinary amazes us with its wonder, mystery and value; the astonishment of love and loving – that too is prayer.

I think also of the vastness of sea or sky, the emptiness of wind; the particularity of a candle, of wild orchids, bog cotton, waving grass; I think of the ruins of a cottage, open to the sky, and a tree growing like a prayer where the hearth once was; I think of a child's trusting hand, a grain of wheat. These images aren't ornaments or labels, they're truths. They are not meaning or interpretation but creation: a special perception that might be called prayer.

Prayer is also heightened awareness and special perception on the part of communities as well as individuals. It can be a communal or corporate activity or response imaged in many ways. We are all human beings first of all and we are human beings in community. Our concern for another person must also be concern for the community in which he or she lives. In our fragmented world we need prayer to hold all that is broken in wholeness and relationship.

Prayer is not a neat and tidy concept. It is a rich, glorious, human, clashing, messy, vibrant, lively mesh of colour. It is not a deliberate setting aside of holy from ordinary but a heightened awareness of the wonder and holiness of ordinary things. Prayer is about life. Why try to make it more – or less? The brokenness, injustice, pain and hurt in our world are not remote from us. We cannot hide from relationship and corporate responsibility in a private, cosy, out-of-this-world holiness.

With all that, maybe we need some sort of ritual, grounding: an act of witness (lighting a candle is one example) as a way of looking at what is broken and fragmented and offering it for, if you like, reconnection; a way of acknowledging that out of messiness and confusion come glorious possibilities. Within this small symbolic act is a dedicated creativity: attention to the small, care for the humble, standing with marginalised people. It awakens the possibility that human hands and hearts will be opened and, through the dedicated creativity (which I might call prayer) of small groups of people, communities and structures may be transformed.

lament ...

Sing a sad song
for the miseries of the world.
Weep with me
tears of passion, anger
and deep regret

for people dying,
unheeded, untended,
from weather, hunger
and the ways of men;
for children crying
where nobody hears;
for people turned away
from places they dream
of calling home;
for people sick and uncared for,
dirty and unkempt;
for people oppressed
and longing for justice.

Sing a sad song
for the miseries of the world.
Weep with me
tears of passion, anger
and deep regret

for the neglect and abuse
of the earth and pollution
of the sweet waters;
for air unfit for breathing;

for memories of bees and fruit
and sweet apple scent;
for the last butterfly
and disappearing paths;
for the fields
covered in tarmac;
for the last puffin
flying into the sunset.

Sing a sad song
for the miseries of the world.
Weep with me
tears of passion, anger
and deep regret

as we walk across a field
in the last light
of a summer evening
sensing the approaching winter
and remember
that out of our awareness,
our knowing, our lamenting
our grieving
will come our hope.

soil and soul

For the sweetness of soil
from which we come
and to which we will return

We give thanks with joy and wonder

For the openness of air
which we breathe
and sometimes walk upon

We give thanks with joy and wonder

For the release of water
that bubbles and streams
and sometimes questions

We give thanks with joy and wonder

For the surprise of fire
that kindles and flames,
is fearsome and bold
and sometimes lights up faces
with laughter

We give thanks with joy and wonder

May we see in these elements
our need, our fulfilment
and our belonging.

yeast that a woman took ...
a story of bread and breadmaking

In Matthew's gospel chapter 13 verse 33 is this highly significant and beautifully positioned (following the parables of the sower and the mustard seed) little story:

> *He told them another parable: 'The kingdom of heaven is like yeast that a woman took and mixed with three measures of flour until all of it was leavened.'*

In the beginning
is the yeast.
This quietest of all possibilities
lives on leaves and tree bark,
in soil and on fruit skins,
in seed and fresh air,
comes from the everywhere.

A woman, the storyteller
of long ago Palestine
tells us, takes this yeast,
and adds to it
three measures of flour.
Tended by time
and a woman's caring
hands, the yeast begins
its all-pervasive activity.
Quietly, gently, it renews,
enlarges, transforms,
irreversibly filling all matter
with anticipation and airiness,
with creative, life-affirming
vitality.

The storyteller sits butterfly light
to life. He makes water into wine
to give the party sweetness
and flavour. He celebrates
the beauty of bread;
pictures its sensual
sculptural, visual pleasure;
touches the moment
when the prospect of a hard grain cake
becomes the possibility
that satisfies
belly, spirit and senses:
the full-bodied
breadiness of bread: purity
in wholeness and joy:
the livingness of life.

And the yeast
holds on to its mystery.

making bread is an elemental activity needing in the right proportions:

earth, that is statement and naming, and soil for bearing plants; air, that is rising and transforming, that is breathing and taking words to make them grow, that knows no frontiers; that is shared. water, that is a quest, a flowing, a search, that is about waves of energy and lakes of stillness. Water, at the temperature of your own body. If it is hotter it will kill the yeast.
fire so deeply embodied in the wonder of creation, that is about the energy to rise, to love – about the doing of bread – what happens around a fire: a meal cooked and shared, stories shared; the command to rise, in the fullness of time.

Being a breadmaker is a good and poetic way to be. It needs time and love. It puts us back in touch with our roots, makes us aware of the sacredness of our earth and its gifts. These are the stuff of bread and poetry, bringing their own stories to the one story, the many ingredients to the One Loaf:

flour – the sweetness of cracked grain, milled from sunlight.
oil – for tenderness and moistness.
Flour and oil: these are the men's gifts.
water – the first gift, flowing through all life, reminding us we are one.
yeast – a plant with a single cell, putting out buds and making more buds, an ever-recurring mystery, needing love and care – a living organism, growing on beer, coming naturally, spontaneously out of the air and from the wheat itself to make sourdough, the culture saved from yesterday's baking. Sourdough bread is the oldest recipe in history, preserved through generations.
salt – to enhance flavour and slow the activity of yeast, to hold

a mystery, a way to remember the many salt tears we weep for home; salt in the sweat of hands that have touched the earth, hands that labour and love.

a little milk – the product of the mother, to give life

a little honey – to give love of life, for good-to-be-alive sweetness and tenderness. Honey tells of a world of sufficiency and sharing. Milk and honey: these are the women's gifts.

sweat – for this milk and honey land is no dream of luxury, no fool's paradise – fleshpots and doing nothing – but a dream of fertility, of honest toil and the sweat of moist hands that shape and feel, kneading together different elements.

time – love of life and our good earth involves patience, makes time an eternity of warm breath, sweet hours … and waiting … guiding the dough … making suggestions, not forcing … waiting until the texture is flesh-like, springy and alive. Breadmaking is a slow art.

May our sowing and gathering,
making and baking,
breaking and sharing,
give energy to our compassion
and hasten the time
when all share in the feasting
and the fun.

(This is useful in a public act of worship as a symbolic making of bread. Different people slowly bring the ingredients, as they are mentioned, to the front of the church. Of course, if there is time really to make bread, that is even better.)

listen to the silence

Here in the quiet is space
to weep:
for depths of poverty
and pinnacles of wealth;
hostility, impersonality
suffering, indifference
and all that harms people
and all living things.

May we be at peace in the stillness
and hear what lies beyond our words.

Here in the quiet is space
to laugh
for the community's raucous energy
and generosity of spirit
for clowns, angels, smiling faces
and all that heals people.

May we be at peace in the stillness
and hear what lies beyond our words.

Here in the quiet is space
for gut level happenings:
grain and water,
yeast and salt,
milk and honey sweetness;
memories and remembrance,
whisperings of a people's pride
and sorrow, kneaded
into our sharing bread.

May we be at peace in the stillness
and hear what lies beyond our words.

Here in the quiet is space
for making, eating, becoming –
an incarnation story
we hold up for others
in the poet's bread
and the people's poems.

prayer (2)

And if I take time
this glad morning
to enjoy the interplay
of light and shadow
on tree bark, to follow
the dancing yellow flames
that outburst every burning bush
and fill the air with scents
of spices not yet known,
or join the lark's abandonment
as it rises to the occasion,
might I know
that this moment
of grace
is what it means
to be alive.

writing the spirit

Whichever way we look at the symbolism in the Pentecost story in Acts 2, it is about a mind-blowing, heart-searching moment. The wind of change challenges and disturbs not only individuals but whole communities. Martin Luther King spoke of *the storm* which will not abate until a just distribution of the fruits of the earth enables all people to live dignified and decent lives. Spirituality does not exist apart from the social context. Look at when and where the story in Acts is set. The spirit's coming is about more than the individual's inner life. It means engagement: what you do with the material part of your life, how you connect with other people, how you relate to other living entities, how you walk on the earth.

Pentecost isn't a once-and-for-all happening but ongoing and energising hope – here, now, in this world, in this place. It's about that which sustains us, enables us, provokes a just anger and arouses compassion. It's about spirit-filled life bursting out of encounter with darkness and suffering, and it is characterised by joy – not the shallow cheeriness of jolly Christians but the deep joy of those who hope and hear the lark's song in the storm.

Living Spirit
help us to hold on to our Pentecost moments
as we walk into the storm.

May we know the value of story, dream and poetry
that tell us of mystery and wonder, joy and pain,
hopes and visions.

May we not be afraid
to imagine life as it is meant to be

for all people;
to live as if the world we long for
were already here.

Living Spirit
help us to hold on to our Pentecost moments
as we walk into the storm.

May we understand what repentance means,
that it is more than restructuring our lives.
May we appreciate where lament
is part of living, a place to express that depth of sorrow
out of which hope will come.

Living Spirit
help us to hold on to our Pentecost moments
as we walk into the storm.

May we have the vision to see that
understanding is different from knowledge,
harsh dogmas make straightjackets of life,
narrow horizons limit compassion
and abstractions often blanket feelings.

Living Spirit
help us to hold on to our Pentecost moments
as we walk into the storm.

May we long for that understanding of prosperity
that is about sharing the good things of life
and realise that growth must be emotional and moral.
Economic growth is no longer an option.

Living Spirit
help us to hold on to our Pentecost moments
as we walk into the storm.

Lead us to ways that hallow all life
and honour compassion and kindness,
ways that ask questions about what we value
and do not dismiss the people's dreams
because they are illogical,
can't pay for themselves,
get in the way of the economic machine
or disturb the slavish devotion to the laws
of supply and demand.

Give us a spirituality of resistance and struggle
that refuses to let injustice have the last word.

Living Spirit
help us to hold on to our Pentecost moments
as we walk into the storm.

my pen

Sometimes I could imagine myself
by candlelight, with a feather pen,
sitting at a small writing desk.
The pen I held as I dreamed
although not so picturesque
was just as basic as a quill
and also had its well of ink
for dipping and thinking.

I wouldn't part with it,
saw my first fountain pen
as a violation of the purity
of the act of writing.

I needed this essential
relationship of pen and ink,
with words and expression

as a key
to the almost lost
stories of the past,
and the unfound images
of the future.

prayer (3)

as the poetry of the quiet people
who may not inherit the earth,
ever
but do it less harm
than some;

who are the essential colours
in the painting of life,

do as they have to
every working day
to ease with their care
our ordinary lives:

bring the milk
and fill the forms,
dig the ground
and do the sums,
ice the cakes
and cut the hair,
serve the food
wash the clothes,

record the deaths
and births and marriages
and bury the dead,

touch each life with care,
gently
as if each one matters
individually,

as they do.

wondering into a story

When they came ashore, they saw a charcoal fire there with fish laid on it, and some bread. Jesus said, 'Bring some of the fish you have caught.' Simon Peter went on board and hauled the net to land; it was full of big fish, a hundred and fifty-three in all; and yet, many as they were, the net was not torn. Jesus said, 'Come and have breakfast.' None of the disciples dared to ask, 'Who are you?' They knew it was the Lord. Jesus came, took the bread and gave it to them and the fish in the same way.

John 21:9-13

Wind is fresh on his face,
water laps at his feet,
a fire is ready
for the fish and bread meal
at the heart of his story.
Alone, he waits on the shore
for the fishers to come.

And they, with a catch
heavier than their dreams,
sail wondering into this story.
His greeting has the wholeness
of bread and poetry.
No word to suggest dogma or creed;
no ninety-nine impossible things
to believe before breakfast
but this one thing:
life ... in all its abundance
... to be savoured and shared:
'Come and have breakfast.'

The gospels are full of stories of shared meals. They are all eye-opening occasions. Bread – solid, smelly, grainy, earthy bread – and fish, caught locally, for this was a fishing community, are frequently eaten. We are being asked to understand an everyday happening just as we ourselves might experience in a bakery, a kitchen, a café, or a fish and chip shop. Eating together, sharing food, especially perhaps sharing bread (which, after all, is the original meaning of the word 'companionship') erases all distinctions between holy and common, sacred and secular, material and spiritual. We are simply sharing the promise of life and strength. That, I feel, is what Jesus meant when he suggested we remember him in the sharing of bread and wine. There is holiness and wonder in all shared meals: a picnic on the beach, a dinner party, shared sandwiches, supper in a kitchen, community lunch, tea together, fish and chips on a bench in the park, food for a journey, a meal on a mountain with thousands or that breakfast by a lake with a few. Our sense of the sacred needs to be enlarged to include it all … ordinary food made whole and holy in the sharing. Our stumbling generosity, our simple actions are good enough to prepare a feast for all people, good enough to change the world. Sharing food is something intimate and mysterious. Maybe it's naïve to think that small groups of people gathered to share ordinary food – to value the food and the sharing – can make a difference … but in the end it's probably the only thing that will.

nicodemus
John 3:1-21

He knows, this man of substance
and intellect, the way of the world,
the way of the mind. He knows theology,
the scriptures. He was raised with the words
around him and has studied truth.

But he can't seem to touch
the poetry of his own humanity
or truth as a way of being
at ease in his own vulnerability.
He is frightened of what he doesn't know,
of imagination's unlimited validity,
of pushing back the boundaries of the possible
and re-dreaming the world.

'What must I do ...'

The answer to his own question
is given on the wind

that blows where it wills

and always surprises.

prayer (4) ...

as broad vision change –
compassion
and where to live it;

as aligning myself

with what matters,
deep places
where living
is mindful.

mary
(John 12:1-8)

Luxurious loving released
in the pouring out
of sweet-scented oil;
essence that defines
a soaring vision:

a moment of awakening,
the alchemy of imagination
heightened colour, sound, movement,
in soft womanliness, the evanescence
of life and quiet grace;
free-flowing hair,
a body of fire
and a mind
on a journey,

beauty remembered for ever
and enough to carry hope
to a broken world.

poppy field

No sense of certainty,
no time for naming,
no awareness of destination
or seeking out a path
to follow but a distant
glimpse, through trees:
so much red: a warning
about the inadequacy of language
and the impurity of description.

a proverbial story

A good year for acorns.
The children love them,
hold them on their palms
looking:

green, yellowing at the tip
as smooth as young fingernails
sits in a cup like a pipe
an old fairy might smoke.

They leave them here
to shrivel unplanted
and take away
possibilities.

underneath are the everlasting arms*
a reflection for mothering sunday

When the wine gave out, the mother of Jesus said to him, 'They have no wine.' And Jesus said to her, 'Woman, what concern is that to you and to me? My hour has not yet come.' His mother said to the servants, 'Do whatever he tells you.'

John 2:3-5 (NRSV)

Meanwhile, standing near the cross of Jesus were his mother, and his mother's sister, Mary the wife of Clopas, and Mary Magdalene. When Jesus saw his mother and the disciple whom he loved standing beside her, he said to his mother, 'Woman, here is your son.' Then he said to the disciple. 'Here is your mother.' And from that hour the disciple took her into his own home.

John 19:25-27

These two passages from John's Gospel are interesting for a number of reasons, not least for what they tell us about the mother/son relationship. We see love and letting go, we see recognition in two people of what relationship means. 'Woman' is a term of respect, and recognises Mary as disciple and compassionate woman. Personal relationship moves out into the world, towards a deeper, more universal understanding. Mother is 'woman' as son has become 'man'. We are seeing the end to which all mothering moves: the human being who has been cherished and nurtured becomes fully mature and human – the moment when both must let go.

---

* Deuteronomy 33:27 (AV)

Our theology has rarely explored mother love or developed the imagery of mothering. We tend to see motherhood as an accumulation of rather mundane and private actions, activities and feelings. So we develop language and imagery around individual mothers but not for that universal concept of mothering at the heart of life and nurture.

Mothering is silent.
Mothering waits.

sisera's mother *

Who does not cast a glance
to where an unnamed mother sits
silently, at the edge of her story?

Pondering in her heart
the things of his growing, she waits,
powerless and voiceless,
for the hoofbeat of his horses
on the soil of home;
while talk is of damsels
and dyed stuff
to grace a victor's neck;

She watches the dawning:
the gradual revealing
of a vast emptiness,
for many share the dying
but few the knowing.

The rays of the morning sun
pierce her heart

and her still body is the shape
of a multitude of grieving women;
for no one asks the mothers
when the talk is of war
and the spoils of war.

* Kings Chapter 5

Mothering of its very nature encompasses the waiting that bridges the gap between being and doing. Mothers have always known about giving of the body, waiting at a birth, as the infant feeds, at the bedside of the dying, for news of missing sons and daughters. There is stillness but there are times when you do not dare look into their eyes (see page)

Mothering is a way of being that cherishes and gives all in relationships one to another and to all life. It is birthing and sustaining, watching and trusting. It waits through winters of suffering for spring and new growth, for resurrection joy.

Reflect for a moment on the rich and often under-used imagery of mothering.

(Silent reflection)

Birthing and beginning,
nurturing and nourishing,
planting and digging,
gathering and harvesting,

we are part of the circle,
of the earth and of each other;

waking, wondering and wandering,
writing poems, telling stories,
shaping, painting and weaving,
exploring language and colour,

we are part of the circle,
of the earth and of each other;

making and living love,
changing nappies, washing floors
baking bread, cooking meals,
touching, smelling, hearing,
sharing, celebrating and sorrowing,

we are part of the circle,
of the earth and of each other;

through the hurting and the healing,
the breaking and the renewal,
the accepting and the letting go,
sthe dying and the ending,

we are part of the circle
of the earth and of each other.

(Silent reflection)

In birth and death
in ebb and flow
the trusting and the cherishing
the unknowing and the uncertainty
the hope and the promise
the worship that is a kiss
in the dark,

we trust the mystery of mothering
and the creativity of nurture.

In the transformation that comes with
conceiving, forming, labouring,
birthing, cherishing and letting go;
in all-day, all-life commitment
the watching and the waiting
the patience and the impatience,

we trust the mystery of mothering
and the creativity of nurture.

In our speech and in our silence,
in the right word at the right time,
the exact moment to hear the story,
our telling and our holding,
our remembering and our forgetting,

we trust the mystery of mothering
and the creativity of nurture.

In hands and hearts
that tend and care
and bring out goodness,
in green shoots,
buds and blossoming,

in the vulnerability of communion
with the gentle gifting earth,

we trust the mystery of mothering
and the creativity of nurture.

In our being and our doing
we rejoice and we lament
the ordinary and the extraordinary

the beautiful and the plain,
creativity and craft,
living and dying,
with open and thankful hearts,

we trust the mystery of mothering
and the creativity of nurture.

In our good dreaming
may we find vision and imagination,
    awe and wonder.
    compassion and commitment,
    fire and vigour

that we may live with uncertainty
  and the deep, hard secret of love.

sacrifice

Isaac asked, 'Here are the fire and the wood, but where is the sheep for a sacrifice?' Abraham answered, 'God will provide himself with a sheep for a sacrifice, my son.'

Genesis 22:7,8 REB

A long struggle you had of it,
Father Abraham; a long journey
reaching its end at the foothills
of a mountain of hope.

All this late in the day,
in the winter of your thought
but there was no escape.
Together you had travelled:
father and son,
innocence of youth
and pride of age
to the appointed place.

The struggle was still alive in you
Father Abraham, holding high the knife.
Innocence and truth, goodness and youth
held and bound, awaited the end
of your seeking: a distant meeting
with Love, all love
love for which an old man's pride
in the god he thought he knew
was adequate sacrifice.

prayer (4)

Be
still and create;
kneel to imagination
when reality dies
and history's bones
are long buried.
Connect in the silence
what you are
with what you
value.

gate to the isles

Eliot almost said
old women should be explorers
and I think of Winifred Nicholson's
Gate to the Isles.
How surprising and life-giving
to go through
the particular blue
and beckoning opening
into a place of impressions,
momentary experiences
and thoughts beyond meaning,
unrecognised ... unless
I tell them.

midwinter fire

At the year's low point
holly, almost invulnerable
it seems, to time and seasons,
gathers the little light.
Its leaves reflect like mirrors
and will burn fiercely
even on living trees.

But its flowers, folk say,
make water freeze
and holly wood thrown
to any animal
will bring it back
quietly.

Holly sprigs were sent to friends
to celebrate the sun god's birth.
When you and I were first in love
we brought in holly from the woods
to make Christmas at home.

Holly trees sprung up
under Christ's footsteps.

Leave it uncut, unshaped
in the hedgerow.
Bad luck, they say
follows its felling
but growing, its goodwill
keeps away witches
and fairy folk.

Deep at the green heart
of this tree of unlikeness
is the blood red energy
of stories and myths:
older than dreams,
younger than tomorrow.

once upon a time ...

In all our words and wonderings,
our choices and rejections,
our beginnings and endings,
may we value rightly
that great collection
of human dreams and visions
we call the Bible.

We celebrate the wonder of many stories
and the joy of the whole story.

May we use imagination
  to read with open minds;
  find life in words;
  become part of the story.

We celebrate the wonder of many stories
and the joy of the whole story.

May we have the insight
  to discern what is good
   discard what is bad
   discover what is hidden;
   dance to life's rhythm
    in poetry and song.

We celebrate the wonder of many stories
and the joy of the whole story.

May we understand
  that the Bible, gifted from the past,
  with power still to move and change,
  may be for us the way,
  not the end, of our dreaming;
  that justice, joy and outspoken love
  may be the hope we release
  from ancient stories
  into today's world.

We celebrate the wonder of many stories
and the joy of the whole story.

trust the story

Nobody was paying attention. Her arguments were sound and she spoke well but nobody seemed interested. Her words fell on stony ground. She paused and started again: 'Once upon a time …,' she said. Suddenly everyone was quiet, everyone was listening, imaginatively paying attention.

'Once upon a time, a princess went for a walk with a dove and a tortoise' … now she had their full imaginative attention …

Everyone loves stories! Storytellers over the centuries have known that people listen when you tell a story. We tell them to help us through our muddles and confusions, to weave threads and make connections. Story somehow transforms situations and people and we see more clearly *how things are*. Fairy tales, especially, are about the wonder of the small, everyday things we see around us and are astonishingly true to life. If you've ever looked at the early morning sun on a tree … seeing the way the light plays on apples … you'll find it difficult to say that these are not magical in the way they are often shown to be in fairy stories.

The success of a story often depends upon small actions and objects: like the shape of a tree or a twist in the road. Tellers of fairy tales make sure we really see things by giving them a life of their own: bread talks, pots and pans move about. And so much is *chance*. Think about how often our future is decided by something as small as a light in a window, a turn in the road, bumping into someone in the street, sharing food … life's like that.

Writer Angela Carter once described fairy tales as stories 'where one king goes to another king to borrow a cup of sugar'. They are a wonderful mix of the magical and the domestic. All sorts of ordinary objects like cooking pots and spoons enchant us.

We share stories to build up relationships with other people. Hearing and telling the world's folk tales, legends, fairy tales helps us sort out our own story and understand that others have their own stories. Remember the tales of the Arabian Nights: Scheherazade tells the king stories to avoid being put to death. She constructs her tales to amuse and intrigue her one-man audience but also to re-dream the world. She puts off death by telling stories to a tyrant and they are both transformed and fall in love. That's the story of storytelling!

Stories are about our hunger for life itself, for we are all made of stories … and as we need good food we need good stories. We tell stories about stories to work out the difference between the good and bad ones; the difference between the stories that give people courage and compassion and those that make them cowardly and careless about love and justice.

Magical tales are all around us. When the first child for half a century was born on Hoy, one of the Orkney Islands, poet George Mackay Brown wrote of her opening her eyes on 'the storied light'. Think how many lights in windows make up our lives.

So in sharing stories we are sharing hope, value and understanding; we are learning to belong. You might think you are too old for fairy stories but remember Hans Christian Andersen wrote, first of all, for adults. His stories, like the parables of Jesus, don't moralise or sermonise but look at life as it is, with all its wonder and uncertainty. He saw his stories as seeds that would grow with each retelling. Being human is all about telling stories and listening to those of others. Think about it: are you old enough for fairy stories again?

the good storyteller

There's a story in Mark's Gospel, chapter 12, verses 1-2 which is very typical of Mark and is more troublesome than it at first appears. It's allegory rather than parable: everything refers to something else: the vineyard is the land, the owner is God, the tenants are religious leaders, God's emissaries are the prophets, the son is Jesus. The action moves to an appointed end and the whole becomes a sort of justification for that transition from the old to the new which is the basis of Mark's gospel.

Mark is confident of God's action in the world and, in almost desperate over-explicitness, allows goodness no human or earthly resting place: 'This is the Lord's doing …' (verse 11)

The focal point of this story is the life of Jesus himself: the rejected cornerstone. That's what disturbs the religious leaders – and no wonder! It's a good story and good stories can change things. Transformation of people and communities begins in the imagination, in telling a story embodying our ideals. Stories work on our immunity to human emotions. They challenge any creed, dogma or religious belief that leaves a community as unjust and oppressive as ever. Religiosity will not avert God's justice.

The human Jesus, the good man, doesn't talk ethics. He tells stories – stories intended to reveal rather than inform; stories that show us how to be alive together.

Those who hear recognise this parable as aimed at them. There is no lack of understanding: bullies must be resisted and the earth (God's vineyard) cherished for all people.

May the story-maker
bless you
with a lifetime of stories
that grow and heal
in their telling

May the dream-maker
bless you with upside down dreams
that compassionately reshape the world

And may all your imaginings
breathe life into failing spirits
and bring hope in troubled times.

prayer (5)

Hold the everyday language
of your doing and being
in an ordinary day.
Savour the words.
Hear the music
they make as they tremble
in your knees, shudder
down your spine
and make the poetry
of your story: personal,
yet telling all the things
of our humanness.

Plant the words,
nurture them
as you might wild flowers
in an exotic garden.

advent sunday 2007
(For Barrie)

For all that has been, thanks.
For all that will be, yes.
Dag Hammarskjöld

The light that in the beginning
raised life from the cold earth
dances in through church windows
to illuminate the surprising
promise of a spoken word:

the way a monk might colour
his manuscript with yellow-gold,
might offer into the long silence
yesterday, today, tomorrow
that are different
and always will be,
might in the alchemy
of imagination
begin an exploration
of the unknowable
beyond the words
on the page
and so script
an affirmation

that is grace enough.

'be worthy of the bread's aroma' Mahmoud Darwish

(For Jan in Israel/Palestine
and Oliver in England)

The story you tell
from far away
is of baking
in unfamiliar ovens,

of children with bread
in their hands, waiting,
quietly offering

a gift to you
whose pockets are full
of pieces of crumbs.

I know another story:
a small boy at my side
at the end of a school day.
He's uneasy with words
but holds out to share
crumbs left in his lunch box
like a few remaining tears
waiting for weeping.

We all shape the story.
'They belong together
– words and bread'*
mingling small meaning
and a sense of eternity:
and what makes us
worthy of memories
held out in cupped hands.

*From 'A pocket full of crumbs', Jan Sutch Pickard

trusting life

to my newborn grandson ...

I want to say
that being human
is as much about poetry
as faith, as much about feet
as soul.

The moments when I see
into the heart of things
have little to do with beliefs
or creeds ... churches, altars
or black-robed priests,
and everything to do with

a story I tell
about the surprises
of ordinary days.

Everything to do
with the brush of daisy petals
against my bare feet,
and the feel of life
in the bread as it rises
in my hands.

Everything to do with the surprise
of love in newborn eyes
staring back at me
from the depths of a self
you will not find
but create as you live
remembering not the moment
of your birth but the wonder
of your life.

There is no religious or moral rule to equal the demands of love. What people will remember of us is not what rules we kept, what creeds we believed, what doctrines we followed, but when we were kind, when we opened our hearts and minds to the sorrows, joys and fears of others and revealed something of our own weaknesses; when we rejoiced with the joyful and walked alongside the sorrowing, when we encouraged the fearful and protected the timid, when we gasped with wonder at a sunset, or expressed joy at the beauty of a flower, when we were hospitable, generous and forgiving, when we were open to the gifts of those seeking our own giftedness, when we made people feel included and valued … both personally and politically. In other words, how we responded and connected.

Sometimes I think what scares some of us most are the ordinary relationships that go beyond the guidelines, rules and creeds of workplace, club and church into the area of discernment, where, as well as knowledge and understanding, we rely on insight, intuition, trust.

Christianity teaches so much about giving, so little about receiving, especially receiving from those we find difficult, or from whom we might even recoil. Yet to receive from those who take us outside our own comfort zone is perhaps essential to our growing wholeness.

We know that it's not only the teachings of Jesus that make his story so significant but what the Gospels tell us of his physical presence: eating, drinking, celebrating, dancing, walking – the poetry of his life and his willingness to trust at the earthy level of apparent weakness. Jesus, the good man, doesn't talk ethics. He lives values and he tells stories that show us how to be alive together. Stories we can trust ... not so much the word become flesh as the flesh become word.

The process of opening up, letting go, trusting ourselves to others, along with exploration of our deep and often hidden thoughts and feelings, involves body and soul wholeness. Look again at the Passion stories, at how much weeping, washing, bleeding, sweating there is. Can you trust yourself to really attend, really look at all this bodiliness, all this nasty breaking of boundaries, all this broken humanness? The story takes us to a place where there's no time for objectivity, a place beyond reason and logic. Don't avert your gaze to look for angels, or theories, or theologies – atonement? penal substitution? If you turn away from the messiness, the physicality, the destroyed flesh, you will begin a process of separating body and mind and heart where it is possible to rationalise any atrocity. This is a moment of fear. It will stretch to the limits our ability to trust in life – all life, not just human life.

Disconnection is one of the great problems of the modern world and the cause of our social, political, spiritual and ecological crisis. We need to reconnect at all levels in a mutually enhancing relationship between humans and the rest of creation. Think for a moment about breathing. It is the very centre of ordinariness – yet this amazingly simple act is, along with food, what gives and sustains life. Think about it: we inspire – breathe in – we receive inspiration to create. Breath is the energy that unites earthling and earth. The rhythm of breathing returns us to and connects us with the earth to which we belong as part of the life-breath of all living things. There is no duality of body and soul but breathed-in unity. Every time we breathe we reaffirm our trust in life. It's us and the earth.

Increasingly, we need to remember that unity of us and the earth when we think about the food that sustains us, how we grow it, how we celebrate it. We don't bring wheat to the altar. We bring bread. This involves sowing the wheat, then tending and harvesting it before sending it to the miller to produce the flour, with which the baker makes the bread. We don't eat abstractions or even nutrients. We eat food from the earth.

Hungry and trusting, we are one with the earth.

But we can no longer be innocent and unthinking in our eating and our breathing. We can no longer look on the earth as the confident 'stewards' we once thought we were. We know what we have done – what we are still doing – through our greed, through our mass production and over-consumption that pollute and lay waste, that create poverty and ugliness on a huge scale. We also *know* what we must do if life on earth in all its fullness and wonder is to be sustained.

But to turn our *knowledge* into the *will to act,* we need poetry. We need to lament – publicly – and out of this we hope will come the restraint and necessary, appropriate action. We need to reaffirm and celebrate our trust, as thinking, loving beings, in what we can give and what our earth can give, trusting ourselves as *part of* the whole, not *the* whole. That is salvation. That is the 'still, sad music of humanity' that the poet Wordsworth heard. When he wrote his poem *Lines Composed a Few Miles above Tintern Abbey* he struggled with unresolved personal ambiguities much as we do but he also saw 'something far more deeply interfused ... that impels/all thinking things, all objects of all thought/and rolls through all things' – Life. And we might see it too, as we watch, for example, a woman sitting in the sun against a stone wall. There is a pattern of connection that is intricate, complex, creative. That is what Wordsworth saw as adequate recompense for loss of the glorious abandon of youth and unknowing.

It's Garden of Eden stuff. It might ask: Can you trust an apple?

Just one bite explodes in her mouth.
Is it too much to want
knowledge and the garden,

sweetness and ashes?
She sees the fruit fall,
   and rot,
the ripe seed die
   in the ground
so that tomorrow
the air may be filled
with the heady scent
of apple blossom.

(from 'Apple Life', Joy Mead, *A Touching Place*)

The stone that holds those things we thought we knew – our dogmas and creeds, our theories and theologies – has been rolled away and we are left with empty space we must learn to trust. At the very heart of many faiths and thought systems is a simplicity which the world needs: an abiding trust in life and the often unpredictable and totally surprising form the expression of love takes in the lives of people living justly and compassionately.

celebrating an ordinary day

As we greet with wonder and uncertainty
the coming and the happenings of this new day

How can we keep from singing.

As we see holiness in ordinary places
where people in all their depth and mystery
work and play, laugh and cry;
where life is cherished, sustained
and handed on

How can we keep from singing.

As we oppose all that denies life
in its fullness and variety;
in our lives, our communities, our world

How can we keep from singing.

As we weep over injustice
rejoice in goodness
love outrageously

How can we keep from singing.

As we affirm our hope for tomorrow
and our faith in the indefinable

How can we keep from singing.

pieces of a life

like the remaining stones
of some ancient building
or an old graveyard.

They are the music
of moments that happened
or might happen,
the daily journey
the mind makes,
a devotion of naming,
remembering, noticing.

Grass blades, spiders' webs, grasshoppers
and the music of fields;
the feather-like shades
of the colours of a room at dusk
and the way stones hold silence:

nothing is inconsequential

because of the grace of memory,
because of imagination,
because of love.

making paths

(For Frances)

We work among your trees
talking as our hands
touch earth and wood.
Spirit, it seems to me,
enters the world
through the wildness
of words, rooted yet branching
unconfined, disobedient
to garden rules, digressing
into the diversity
of conversation.

What we plant usually outwits us
and will surely outlive us, growing
gently over our attempts
to make a way
through the woods.

Grassy glades offer pauses
like the silence of night
in a forest of changing
perceptions.

Memory becomes the way to beauty
made by walking the path home.

on the road

to the North End
he stops to say:

How strange to look
and not to see
the Abbey at all.

I turn to face
the melted whiteness
of a shroud,
the haunting secrecy
of what I can't see
and find I long
to be let through
to what I know
is there.

prayer (6)

It's a route
that's indirect,
a way half-remembered
going nowhere,
with nobody,
a path that suddenly
comes upon a clearing
of sunlight and shadows,
an always-changing place,
of many meanings
and no meaning.

The rootedness, the particular thing
that joins the earth to the words I use,
can't be approached
in any usual way.
It has need of wings.

famine road

When you and I follow the map
and meet the unnecessary road
that trails away to nothing
the earth beneath our feet
is strangely sweet with gentians
– a blue so intense
no camera or searching mind
could accurately
hold the colour.

Each of the following four poems was written for a grandchild at his or her birth. They are faith songs, celebrations of new life and expressions of awe and wonder at the coming of new life, the great creative force in which we share. They are specific to the child and occasion concerned but could be used for others, with adaptation, or might suggest a way to create your own celebrations.

a welcome for william

Born 17th May, 2001

Let buds burst open
and flowers turn to the rising sun.

Let wind caress our faces
with surprises
and rustle the trees
with expectation.

Let hidden corners of the world
be washed clean and fresh
by gentle rain.

Let children run and shout and jump
and larks fill the air with music
as sweet as our dreams.

Let old people watch
new beginnings
with smiles and hopes.

Let lambs leap
and dogs chase their tails.
Let kites and balloons garland
a cloudless sky.

Let the sound of celebration
from fête and funfair,
concert hall and park
fill the air
of this given day.

Let rainbows colour the sky
with promises,
trees wave,
stones stand firm.

Let bread be broken
and enjoyed with friends,
candles be lit
and cakes cut.

Let wishes come true.

Let you and I hold
our own and our children's
childhoods in our open hearts.
Let us wonder at the air
we walk on today.

For new eyes have opened
on the dawning.
Tiny fingers have reached out
and touched
old hearts grown wise
from looking at fragility:
all this littleness
come to give us tomorrow
today.

emily's song

One day you look over a river
far inland, thinking fish, not seals
and then one appears – a seal *
one of the magic creatures,
a surprising messenger
on its own journey

bringing music of the sea,
laughter of the waves,
secret sounds from faraway places
that stay in the heart long after
we can hear them no more;
bringing a blessing
for Emily
whose eyes are newly opened
on the mysteries of the world.

Legend says that there's a seal out at sea
for each human life walking the earth
and people might sing
to the crooning seal
'Come ashore, come ashore,
come ... to us.'
And maybe this is why
it's as if she has always been

somewhere – waiting
for a sea song of welcome;
it's as if we'd always known
she would come –
like looking out to the rocks
thinking there are no seals.
Then hearing their haunting song,
knowing they are there
waiting.

* Around the time of Emily's birth on 2nd April 2002 a seal appeared in the River Ouse above York – a long way from the sea!

summer song

(For Alasdair, born 20th June, 2003)

Almost midsummer, the days long,
the woods green and quiet.
There is warmth in the earth
and no whistling wind
to worry the long days:
a good season for travelling,
to set out on the longest
of all journeys.

You come at a time sweetened
by the sun,
between its golden setting
on a mothy evening
and the first light of morning
which leaves its sparkle
in your newly opened eyes.
This first light of morning
is to you all magical movements –
angels and ghosts
sunbeams and shadows –
a world waiting
to be coloured in.

I see in your perfect little face
a fragile wonder, a promise
hidden in the tomorrow
of your unmade smile
– a sunburst
waiting to happen.

oliver

(For my grandson – born 24th June 2004,
while I was at the St Magnus Festival on Orkney)

As if the wind that blew across Orkney
all that long week before your birth;

as if the deep and unfathomable blue
of sea and sky
and the huge light
of these islands;

as if the yellow
of fields full of buttercups,
the wild joy of larks rising
and the haunting calls
of curlews and oystercatchers;

as if the days full of music
and the air that holds it;

as if the smiles of the people
in shops and cafes, concert halls and churches;

as if the held joy
of days of waiting
and awareness of the faraway
space where you were not

are all gathered
in this moment
as I feel the weight of you,
just a little more
than not being here,
a little heavier
than the air I breathe
and think to walk upon.

seven blessings

A first blessing is your meeting
with friend and with stranger;
a second blessing is breaking
the bread of your belonging;
a third blessing is preparing you,
freeing and furthering you;
a fourth blessing is homing you
in the space that is yours;
a fifth blessing is the silence
that holds you in unknowing;
a sixth blessing is the attention
that's given to each moment;
a seventh blessing is the wondering
that sanctifies your becoming.

ordinary, particular, universal

What do worship, miracle, praise mean
if not seeing as if for the first time
the particular way evening sunlight
touches the edge of the garden

or waiting on a day
of great delight
to see dolphins

or the sustaining memories
brought back to my mother
as she held in her arms
her first great grandson

or at the end of a week
of conversation, celebration, challenge
walking together, old friends,
the three of us in the sun
towards the sand and the sea
at the edge of the island –
alive to each
particular joy

wordlessly knowing

the way things are.

uncovering more ...

A boat emerging from tarpaulin
at the beginning of summer,
a child's open face, waiting,
the washing machine in action
cabbages beautiful in garden rows,
gannets over the sea,
lights in my neighbour's window
the lasting colour of birch leaves
at the end of autumn,

the location,
the naming
the remembering,

the music of our daily being
where nothing is inconsequential
but sometimes may be too late.

Not searching for meaning
but a way of telling
the everyday actions
of ordinary people
made visionary
because of love.

How rituals are created
and myths are made.

notes

The poem and bread-making reflection on pages 112-113 come from my book *The One Loaf*.
Sisera's mother on pages 129 comes from *A Telling Place*.
To my newborn grandson on page 145 comes from *Where Are the Altars?*

All published by Wild Goose Publications, www.ionabooks.com

As always, my thanks to everyone at Wild Goose publications and especially Sandra for the kindly, conscientious and efficient way she handles the writing and the writer. Thank you too to Stephen Raw (StephenRaw.com) for more beautiful cover artwork.

wild goose publications is part of the iona community:

- An ecumenical movement of men and women from different walks of life and different traditions in the Christian church
- Committed to the gospel of Jesus Christ, and to following where that leads, even into the unknown
- Engaged together, and with people of goodwill across the world, in acting, reflecting and praying for justice, peace and the integrity of creation
- Convinced that the inclusive community we seek must be embodied in the community we practise

Together with our staff, we are responsible for:

- Our islands residential centres of Iona Abbey, the MacLeod Centre on Iona, and Camas Adventure Centre on the Ross of Mull

and in Glasgow:

- The administration of the Community
- Our work with young people
- Our publishing house, Wild Goose Publications
- Our association in the revitalising of worship with the Wild Goose Resource Group

The Iona Community was founded in Glasgow in 1938 by George MacLeod, minister, visionary and prophetic witness for peace, in the context of the poverty and despair of the Depression. Its original task of rebuilding the monastic ruins of Iona Abbey became a sign of hopeful rebuilding of community in Scotland and beyond. Today, we are about 270 members, mostly in Britain, and about 1500 associate members, with over a thousand friends worldwide. Together and apart, 'we follow the light we have, and pray for more light'.

For information on the Iona Community contact:
The Iona Community, Fourth Floor, Savoy House, 140 Sauchiehall Street, Glasgow G2 3DH, UK. Phone: 0141 332 6343
e-mail: admin@iona.org.uk; web: www.iona.org.uk

For enquiries about visiting Iona, please contact:
Iona Abbey, Isle of Iona, Argyll PA76 6SN, UK. Phone: 01681 700404
e-mail: ionacomm@iona.org.uk

Wild Goose Publications, the publishing house of the Iona Community established in the Celtic Christian tradition of Saint Columba, produces books, e-books, CDs and digital downloads on:

- holistic spirituality
- social justice
- political and peace issues
- healing
- innovative approaches to worship
- song in worship, including the work of the Wild Goose Resource Group
- material for meditation and reflection

For more information:

Wild Goose Publications
Fourth Floor, Savoy House
140 Sauchiehall Street,
Glasgow G2 3DH, UK

Tel. +44 (0)141 332 6292
Fax +44 (0)141 332 1090
e-mail: admin@ionabooks.com

or visit our website at
www.ionabooks.com
for details of all our products and online sales